THE ELEMENTS
BY RICKY GOODALL

The Elements

Copyright © 2015 Ricky Goodall

Cover Art: Anthony Manuele
Graph in Creative Visualization: Ekaterina Reymarova
Formatted by IRONHORSE Formatting

ISBN-13: 978-0-9947263-0-8

This book is dedicated to you, the reader.

I wrote it to help manifest your dreams

and by reading it, you're helping manifest mine.

ACKNOWLEDGMENTS

I'm incredibly grateful to have so many people to thank. I hope to remember as many as I can, and you know I love you all, so there's no order of importance. I will start with a special thanks to Leslie Gallagher, who was the first of three people to come through at the very end of my Kickstarter campaign to have this book published. Joining her would be Scott Lewis and Martin Blais. You three are directly responsible for making this book possible. Thank you!

I'd also like to thank New York Times bestselling author, Cathryn Fox, for acting as a mentor through the publication process of this book. Your help is much appreciated!

Next, I want to thank my parents for always believing in me, being proud of me, and preparing me for the world ahead.

As silly as it may sound, I realized through my journey that my parents are just people, too. In fact, at age thirty—which I am right now—my father already had my brother and me and was doing his best to teach us how to be little men from the start. Dad, you were my first martial arts teacher, you showed me how to throw a punch and you taught me that when someone hits you, you hit him back twice as hard. You were my first influence for nutrition, fitness, speaking politely, working hard, and so much more. You taught me how to present myself to others and when to keep my mouth shut. I love you, Dad.

Mom, you taught me how to read and write at such a young age that it opened an entire world to me. You were, and still are, endlessly helpful and forgiving. I suppose you learn that when you raise boys. You might have been a bit easier on Joey, but I know it was because you always knew what I had in me. I love you, Mom.

I want to thank my brother for always making me feel good about being a big brother. He was my first guitar teacher, my first martial arts training partner, and despite what he may think, he's always been a little bit tougher and just a little bit braver. We've had our hard times, but there's a reason everyone says we look alike; we're not all that different. I love you, Joey.

Lisa, my lovely sister... We might drive each other crazy, but like Joey and I, we're not all that different. I love you, and it's a pleasure to be your brother.

I want to thank some of my best friends, too, who have had a tremendous part in this journey. I want to thank Alden for being a brother to me for all of these years and leading me as much as you've followed me. You have believed in me and been there for me more than anyone else I've ever known. I love you more than words.

Anthony, I think you know how much you meant to this book. You're probably sending me a text message, interrupting me as I write these words. I'm continually amused by our ability to balance one another and not ever all that surprised when we're thinking the same thoughts and experiencing the same peaks and valleys. You have been one of the most influential and truly beautiful parts of my life that I am forever grateful for. It's a pleasure to co-create with you.

To my big brother from another mother, Robbie, who is

anything but big: We've been through so much, and you've been a mentor, a leader, a brother, a coach, and a friend, no matter how bad it got. Remembering what you've done for me always brings a lump to my throat. I love you, man.

Luke, wow where has the time gone? It's funny, we always said we'd end up with beautiful, dark-haired dream girls; I think we were on to something. You have also been a big brother to me, helping me learn self-respect while showing compassion and empathy. You, Shad, and Dougie will always be something special to me.

I'd like to thank my friend, Adam, who introduced me to Reiki and has been a continual supporter of everything I do, just as I am for him. Adam is yet another multitalented guy who has much to offer the world.

Big thanks to my new business partner, Scott, who is teaching me far more than he thinks I teach him. A hungry, self-motivating personal trainer and soon-to-be trailblazing thought leader who is sure to make big waves. Keep an eye out for this guy.

Ghislain is a guest writer in the chapter The Underworld and an incredibly sharp guy. Thanks for everything within and outside of this book.

To my first business partner and very close friend, Andrew, who supported my dreams and was one of the first people to take a big chance on me, I give huge thanks. You have and continue to be one of my biggest supporters.

To all of my teammates, from Titans in New Glasgow and Halifax to my new home, Forca MMA: No matter where we've all been or what we've been through, we'll always be brothers (and sisters) in arms. Oss.

Finally, saving the best for last— my lovely partner and soul mate, Ekaterina. Thank you for always believing in me, keeping me focused on the journey, and offering me a hope in partnerships that no one could. You continue to amaze me with every day and every breath. I love you, Kat.

I have an incredible life full of incredible people, and I could easily fill this book with people to thank. The energy we invest into our community will always pay off in dividends, through abundance and happiness beyond our comprehension, and my life continues to be living proof of it.

Lastly, I thank you, the reader, for blessing me with your attention and time and offering me the chance to live my dream while helping you create yours. I hope this book stimulates your mind and touches your heart.

Yours Truly,

Ricky Goodall

CONTENTS

About The Author

Ricky Goodall was born in Halifax, NS on February 8, 1984. He lived in Dartmouth, NS until he was nine years old, moved to New Glasgow, NS until he finished high school, then moved back to Halifax. Besides writing, Ricky has also trained martial arts since he was thirteen years old, including Karate, Kickboxing, and Brazilian Jiu Jitsu, and eventually became a professional mixed martial artist. He has competed twenty-one times across Canada, eight times on television. Ricky's other passions include playing music (guitar, drums, and singing), business, and wellness.

Ricky currently works with various community projects including Phoenix Youth Programs, Community Carrot, and Plan Canada, and frequently donates to various charities at www.canadahelps.org. One hundred percent of this book's profits are donated to Phoenix Youth Programs.

Visit the links below to check out some of Ricky's other projects:

Ricky's YouTube Channel
www.youtube.com/higherlevelpotential

Ricky's Website www.rickygoodall.com

The Nutrition Blueprint www.thenutritionblueprint.com

Elevated Wellness Center www.elevatedwellness.org

INTRODUCTION

Despite only being thirty years old, I've had a bit of a colorful life, at least so far. I've opened four businesses, all with basically no money and no credit. I've fought twenty-one mixed martial arts fights across my country, Canada. I've appeared on reality television shows, have taught as a college instructor (with no formal experience), and performed music about a hundred times. I've also coached nearly five hundred clients in nutrition, traveled to a few countries, partied with rock stars, and dated models.

I'm not telling you this stuff to impress you. Frankly, knowing what I know now, I think I could have done a lot more. I'm telling you this because I've figured out the necessities to make my dreams come true, and this book is about just that. But before we get there, I should tell you how it all started.

I grew up in Dartmouth, Nova Scotia, with my mother, father, and younger brother, Joey. Throughout most of our childhood we were poor, though in the earlier years, it was up and down. I spent a lot of my younger years in foster care until eventually moving out on my own at fifteen years old.

From around eighteen years old to twenty-two years old, I had a typical, late teen-early twenties life. I started and dropped out of university, did a lot of eating crap and drinking, weighed a little over two hundred fifty pounds, and by the time I was twenty-two years old, I was homeless and jobless. I balanced my efforts between storing my food bank groceries in friend's houses and tricking fast food workers to give me free food that they "forgot in my drive thru order", even though I didn't have a car.

It was around this time in my life my lifelong best friend, Alden, introduced me to the movie *The Secret*. The movie promised the sun and the moon with everything in between. I remember getting excited about it for a while, and I actually started seeing some success. Little things would happen that couldn't be explained, and it seemed that life started to change a bit.

At twenty-three years old, still two hundred fifty pounds, I decided on a five- week notice to fight my first ever mixed martial arts fight under the Pictou County Titans. I trained twice a day, ate barely anything, and lost nearly fifty pounds to weigh in at two hundred pounds against a tall, lean, six-feet-three opponent with kickboxing experience. Despite being the underdog and nearly getting knocked out in the first round, I ended up winning the fight by decision. Ricky Goodall the MMA fighter was born.

SIDENOTE: For those of you who don't know what mixed martial arts is, it's the stuff you might see on television where two men fight with very small gloves in a metal cage. Yes, it's just as crazy as it sounds.

By this time, I'd been living with a girlfriend who had three kids of her own for a year or so. I met her when I was nineteen, and it lasted nearly five years off and on. The relationship was a mix of love, frustration, and anger, and about a year after my first fight, we split up for the last time. With a desire for change, I decided to move from New Glasgow back to Halifax to train with one of the best mixed martial arts clubs in Canada—an affiliate of my hometown team, Titans MMA.

Between the ages of twenty-four and twenty-seven, my life was a balancing act of working in bars as a bouncer, fighting mixed martial arts, finally going to business school, and graduating in marketing. Growing up as a shy kid, I took this opportunity of living in a new city as my chance to rebuild, dig deep into my personal development, and make something of myself. I'd read books on sales, success, confidence, socializing, and even on dating women. There was nothing I wasn't willing to learn if it meant bringing me to a higher level of my own potential. Things were good.

I ended up dating a girl for a couple of years, and as the relationship came to an end, I found myself in the same place as when all of the rest of my relationships ended—miserable, self-loathing, and broken.

Before long, I found myself drinking heavily and headed down a dark path of self-destruction and emotional turmoil. I felt like every bit of pain I had experienced in my life was all coming down on me. No matter how long I cried or how much I tried to busy myself, I couldn't ease it. Rather than give the break-up space and let it settle, I drove my ex-girlfriend completely crazy trying to mend the broken relationship. I couldn't accept it was over; I felt like I was losing a part of myself.

I'm not sure if it was completely out of desperation to find a way to get us back together or my intuition leading me, but I started to remember the movie The Secret and the things I had learned about it years before. There was an entire community based around the concepts of the law of attraction, and a lot more information available than when I first was introduced. It seemed there were more techniques and ideas to be found if a person looked hard enough.

I should tell you that this book isn't about the law of attraction, though. At least, not like you might think it to be.

One of the techniques I found most interesting was meditation. I started to find lots of information suggesting that meditation was one of the most effective techniques in attracting our desires and changing our lives. This piqued my interest even further and sent me down another path.

I remembered Alden trying to teach me meditation a long time before, but I just couldn't learn it, no matter how hard I had tried. I didn't have the determination then. After much frustration, fifteen hundred dollars, and a four-day, intensive Transcendental Meditation course, I finally learned how to meditate. Twice a day, for weeks, I meditated, hoping to attract all of the things I was missing in my life.

There's a funny thing about meditation. When you're left alone with only your own consciousness, working your best to not chase the rabbit of your own distracting thoughts, you start to learn things about yourself. Old patterns emerge, and you begin to see some of your own truths clearly. I started to realize I had a lot of work to do on myself if I expected to be happy in my life, so that's exactly what I did.

In the months to come, I spent time reading personal development books and working with alternative healing modalities like Reiki and Emotional Freedom Technique (EFT), hypnotism, and much more. I started to dig up the patterns of my past and find out what blocks were holding me in that dark place. I started to remove them from my subconscious mind.

Before too long, I realized that the anxiety, fear, and pain I felt in my break-up—and most of my break-ups before—was a deep wound from when I was only nine years old and sent to foster care. I realized the child inside was still afraid to be abandoned by those he loved, and when I faced a perfectly normal and healthy relationship transition in my life, I attributed it to the same pain and loneliness I'd experienced so many years ago.

Until that point, my relationships had been a repeating pattern of dependency, attachment, and fear, rather than enjoyment and love. I realized that the reason for the pain was seldom the relationship or even the person that I was hurt over; in fact they had little to do with it. It was something I was holding inside, and knowing that meant I could do something about it.

The freedom I felt from that realization was like nothing I had ever felt before. All of the sudden, all of my fears, worries, and anxieties disappeared. I started to see things differently in my life and felt the desire to dig a little deeper and see what other gems of information I could find. As this was happening, things around me really started to change. My business was flourishing, incredible opportunities were coming out of nowhere, and it seemed my mind was clear, focused, and driven. Everywhere I went, people greeted me with a warm welcome, money troubles were few and far between, and I felt a real compassion for myself and the world around me. As I started to understand my fears and limiting beliefs, I challenged them, and as a result, my world changed.

What I didn't realize was the path I was headed down was teaching me the secrets to unlocking my own potential and creating the life of my dreams. I was learning how to change my thinking, expand my awareness, and shift my perceptions to allow incredible things to manifest. The more I learned and faced my own inhibitions, the more amazing things got around me. My friendships were incredible, my romantic relationships—when needing to end—ended well, and the fear that had imprisoned me was gone. I was free.

I started to notice patterns in my environment and realized my thoughts were often parallel with my experiences. I would think of someone then run into them shortly after, I would imagine the next car I'd like to own, and one would pass me. It seemed my internal world was starting to show itself in my external environment.

As if it were divine timing, I found myself surrounded by others who shared these types of experiences, including one of my closest friends to date, Anthony Manuele. Besides Alden, Anthony would serve to be the most influential aspect of my dreamscaping journey, continually sharing the roles of teacher and student as we discovered new and old theories and concepts in the way of the world. It turns out, the things we were starting to experience weren't all that new. In fact, there are records of similar experiences dating back thousands of years. The idea of our internal state affecting the world around us was old news.

As the months went on and I really began to do heavy research into these concepts, I started to recognize even more patterns and trends, showing me that there really was a technique to this whole thing. There is a method to manifesting the world around us, and we were discovering its inner workings. As I started to map out the information I was finding, I realized most of it could be grouped into separate sections; seven, to be exact. I realized these groups were the elemental necessities to manifest our desires and live the life of our dreams.

Before too long, it became a fun game, limited only by our expectations. Money, relationships, travel, happiness, excitement, passion; it was all there, and there was plenty of it. Don't get me wrong; there were and are still ups and downs, but for the past eighteen months, I have not lived a day without love or excitement. I have not lived a day clouded by emotional pain and fear.

I have found a trend in my research, a cluster of valuable information I have categorized into seven elemental groups, which I call The Elements.

FOREWORD

When I decided to write this book I knew I had my work cut out
for me. If you're going to tell people you can help them make
their dreams come true, you better damn well be able to.
Luckily for me, and hopefully for you, I truly feel I can.

This book is going to dive into a lot of complex ideas. I can
assure you that although I use a lot of my own language and
describe the concepts in the way I understand them to be, there
are very few original, authentic ideas in this book. In fact, I can't
really take credit for anything other than simply arranging the
concepts in a manner that hopefully makes it easier to
understand. This book is a product of hundreds of hours of
research, including countless videos, articles, books, and
conversations, and an almost obsessive need to share them
with others. This book is a collection of information that is freely
and abundantly available to anyone with the desire to find it.

Though I wrote this book in under three months, and the
majority of the grunt work happened in less than eighteen
months, the full story begins at my birth. There is no aspect of
my life, no matter how good or seemingly bad, that didn't assist
in this book's creation. The first time I realized that I was almost
overwhelmed with emotion. The relief and understanding that
everything I've ever gone through had lead to this incredible,
endlessly beautiful gift of life I experience every day is so
intoxicating that sometimes I get lost in its very essence.

I'd like to go over some housekeeping items before I let you get started. First of all, you might want to think of this book as my *hypothetical*. By definition, a hypothetical is used to explore aspects of a concept but cannot convey the whole of it. Oftentimes, people try to discredit a concept by poking holes in the hypothetical, but in reality, that is an act of theoretical bullying. So to be clear, I'm not claiming anything in this book to be *fact*. In fact, I'm not so sure anything in reality can be proven as such. My understanding is that a fact is something we've accepted not because it has been proven, but rather because of its inability to be unproven. In that case, a fact is simply a theory that believes its own hype.

It's highly likely that some readers may have already, consciously or unconsciously, used many of these concepts to find success in their lives. It's sort of like how some people spend their whole lives learning how to run fast while others seem like "naturals". Regardless, even the fastest natural runners can find value in better understanding and practicing their skill.

I use a lot of different terms in this book—manifestation, dreamscaping, quantum shifting and some others—that get explained as we go. We'll discuss quantum shifting in the final couple of chapters, but I'll clarify the other two now. When I use the word *manifest*, or its derivatives, I'm referring to the actual materialization of a scenario. If your desire is to own a new car, then the *manifestation* of that desire would be when you own the car. When I refer to *manifesting* a desire, I'm referring to the process of having it actualize into our experience. In the case of a new car, it might be coming into some extra money, getting a driver's license, or getting a promotion. All of these instances might lend to the ability to manifest your desire of having a new car. Manifesting may also be understood as actualizing or aligning with something you desire.

Dreamscaping is a term my friend Anthony and I have used to describe actually creating our dreams. It's akin to painting a picture, except the picture is actually our experience of reality. In other words, dreamscaping is the *art* of making our dreams come true.

Most of the concepts I present in this book seem far-fetched and probably downright ridiculous. I was a skeptic, too, at first, as were many of my closest friends and family. However, now that I've experienced all I have, skepticism often reminds of the four-minute mile. Before Roger Bannister ran the four-minute mile, few in the world ever believed it was possible, yet in the last fifty years, it's been lowered by almost seventeen seconds. Once he showed the world that it could be done, and people began to *believe* it to be possible, then all of the sudden, it became an attainable desire. For the many people who subscribe to the ideas in this book, the four-minute mile is just one of the many desires that are available to any who are willing to believe.

If there was one thing I could to tell you to bring with you throughout this book—and your entire life, for that matter—it would be your imagination. Unfortunately, many of us have had our imagination repressed and buried too early in our childhood, and we may believe it's gone forever, but I promise you it is very much alive and available within you. Use your imagination every chance you get; it is your most powerful tool, and if you use it, you have to use it wisely. Imagine only the circumstances and situations you wish to experience, and use it to ponder ideas where there may be missing pieces. No matter what happens in your life, never stop imagining.

A Word on the Law of Attraction

In case you're wondering, some of the ideas in this book were inspired by the law of attraction. It shares many parallels with The Elements and although some concepts may be similar you'll learn in The Shift that the law of attraction is more like a *physical representation of a non-physical event.*

Whatever your stance on it, it's not necessary to believe or not believe it for The Elements to work for you. All you need to do is read the chapters and do the homework, and you *will* manifest your deepest desires.

Do Your Homework

At the end of each chapter, you're going to see homework. The homework comes in two levels: Curious Creator and Master Manifestor. Although it's not necessary to do all homework, it is very important that you at least do the Curious Creator level. Accountability and perseverance are a huge aspect of manifesting our dreams. I've done each of these things through my journey, and they are the reason my dreams continue to manifest.

What Are The Elements?

Each of us has within us the necessary elements of manifestation—the building blocks which determine our ability to influence the quality of our life experience. The problem is few of us know these elements exist, and even fewer know how to use them. Unlike physical matter, the elements aren't something you can find and carry with you. Rather, they are something you must continually search for, refine, and *practice.* These elements shift, move, and dance as we go through our day-to-day lives. They move as we move and grow as we grow.

Much like a doctor doesn't *do* medicine, we can't *do* the elements. By *practicing* the elements, we don't find the ability to manifest our dreams; rather, we find that the ability was always there. Through practice we live the life of our wildest dreams. We become free.

DISCOVER THE ELEMENTS

The next seven chapters represent the elemental necessities required to manifest the life of our dreams. The information can be applied to any culture, any ethnicity, any religion, and anyone—regardless of personal history. We're all able to use this information and it is our birthright to do so.

If you find challenge in seeing the connection between any of the material and your ability to create your dreams, I ask that you continue reading; the answers will come.

I invite you to open your mind and unlock your imagination as I give you The Elements.

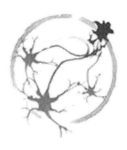

"Belief is the death of intelligence."

– Robert Anton Wilson

ELEMENT 1

EMOTIONAL SELF

Our emotional self can be understood as our entire psychological and emotional make up. It is the foundation of our very existence and heavily determines our ability to actualize our dreams. It is a composition that includes our beliefs, fears, understandings, insecurities, and perspectives on the world around us. When you get nervous before a job interview or get excited to unwrap a gift, this is your emotional self at work. The design of our emotional self comes from many influences, including past experiences, both personally and empathetically, as well as the beliefs we've formed about the perception of those experiences.

How Beliefs Are Formed

A tricky place to be is in the difference between believing something and knowing it. A belief can be engrained so deeply in our psyche that we actually pass it off as something we know. A basic example might be the place we put our keys most of the time. Some of us might have a place we typically leave our keys when we get home. Day after day of putting them in the same spot almost causes us to believe that we *know* where our keys will be when we need them. But can we ever really know for sure? No, we can't. Not until we actually check for our keys, we ever *know* for sure.

With this in mind, we might ask, what are beliefs? Where do they come from, and how are they formed?

Humans are complex and cunning creatures. For thousands of years, hunters have been able to walk through the thickest, deepest woods and find distinct animal tracks. We have looked out into fields and have been able to spot a predator or prey from hundreds of feet away. We've used our attention to detail, laser-sharp focus, and creative imagination to completely dominate the planet as the alpha species.

For hundreds of thousands of years, we humans have relied on our ability to think fast, crunch data, and problem solve on a whim. We've developed highly complex, computational systems in our minds to make educated life or death decisions at the drop of a hat. We've created the ability to look out into what appears to be a calm lake and spot the subtle ripples of water showing us where our next meal is swimming around. This incredibly useful skill can be understood as pattern matching.

The act of pattern matching can be simplified by the imagining following. Some of us, growing up curious and maybe even brave, have done some not so smart things, such as putting our hand on a hot stove burner. After making contact, with an almost unconscious, lightning fast reaction, we've ripped our hands away, hopefully saving ourselves from permanent damage. As we're crying in our mother's arms, a new neural pathway is forged in our subconscious minds assisting in our future survival. This pathway reinforces the belief that touching a hot burner will cause serious pain, and it seldom takes any convincing to believe it to be so. In the future, when we start to subconsciously recognize a similar pattern, perhaps while we're cleaning our stove, our brain matches that pattern to the traumatic event we experienced in childhood, and our internal alarm system starts to go off. The neural pathway can become engrained so deeply that we feel almost the same emotions we felt in the original event before a new one has even occurred. This process of forging neural pathways and recognizing patterns helps us use our conscious minds for other uses, rather than continually being bombarded with decisions. It helps us make instinctive decisions that will usually assist in our survival.

Another trait that assists in human survival is our social capacity. We've developed a strong sense of empathy toward our fellow man. This helps us strengthen relationships, develop tight-knit communities, and adds to the strength of our race. However, sometimes our empathy doesn't serve us so well. In a world full of reality television, drama-filled breaking news reports, and a seemingly endless showcasing of chaos, we've allowed our empathy to create beliefs and fears that we haven't even personally experienced. We've watched other people's lives be affected by a stimulus and created our own beliefs from it.

Of course, the entire evolution of the human race could arguably be attributed to our social dynamic. The sharing of information through personal experience has created patterns many of us thrive on. But what about when the pathways we've created and the patterns we're matching no longer serve us? A pathway we've created in our childhood may be redundant or even counterproductive in our adult life. In fact, a pathway from last week may also not serve us anymore. Throughout our lives, we've created countless pathways and matched limitless patterns that were based on a situation that may be completely invalid today. Here's an example:

Let's imagine that you're playing the leading role of Hamlet in junior high school. You've had a little bit of experience being in front of crowds, but for the most part, you're nervous. You're worried that you're going to completely embarrass yourself in front of the entire school, and none of the other students will ever let it go. Just before you're about to go on stage, one of the other kids trips you, and you stumble recklessly, crashing all of the stage props. You're so incredibly embarrassed that you rush off stage and swear to never perform again.

You've now created a neural pathway in your mind that suggests performing on stage results in embarrassment and perhaps even intense emotional pain. You've filed the pattern you experienced as a traumatic event, and anytime you start to recognize similar patterns, you begin to panic. Your hands get sweaty, your eyes get blurry, and you completely dissolve the idea of ever performing again.

Let's fast forward ten years. You're now in the process of being promoted to the perfect position at your job. This position allows you to make your own schedule, work from home, receive four weeks paid vacation, and offers almost double your salary. The only catch is, in order to get promoted to this position; you need to present a forty-minute proposal to the upper management about why you're fit for the position. You know in your heart that there is no one inside or outside of the company that fits this position better than you, and you know that you have not only the talent but the passion to excel. Still, the fear of getting up and performing in front of your peers completely paralyzes you.

So what do you do? Do you give up on the idea of the job, accepting that you have a fear that can't be overcome? Or do you dig a bit deeper and try to overcome that fear?

Jack Canfield has a great quote; it's one of my all time favorites. He says, "Everything you want is on the other side of fear." Throughout my life, I've experienced an abundance of fearful situations. Every fight I've ever had, every speech I've ever conducted, every job interview I've been in offered some level of fear. As I get older and I experience these situations more and more, I realize that there is no promise land where the fear stops. There is no place you can get to where the fear is gone.

As I mentioned in my introduction, I won my first MMA fight by decision. What I didn't mention was that it was two years later when fought my second, and I lost in the first round. For two years, I held this idea of who I was in my mind so tightly that it morphed into a fear of failure, and in my second fight, I actualized that fear into a loss. A few months later I was set to fight my third fight. I'd enjoyed the rush of winning and felt the sting of losing. For an hour or two before the fight was about to happen, I sat in the locker room, more afraid than I've ever been for any fight since. I was absolutely terrified and kept telling myself *this is it, I'm never going to fight ever again*. I just couldn't handle it. The pressure was too much. It wasn't the opponent I was afraid of—though he was a monster of a man—it was the fear of failure. Or more importantly, it was fear and fear alone.

Despite being scared to death, I went out and fought anyway. I got hurt in the first few minutes of the fight, but I turned it around and ended up winning by submission in the first round. I took the fear I had and transmuted it into an instinctive drive to achieve what I had set out to achieve.

Though the fear I felt before that fight is nothing like any fear I've felt since, the point here is that the fear has never gone away. The fear continues to exist. The only thing that changes is how we react to our fears and what we decide to do about them. Through overcoming that immense fear, I was able to set a new standard for the level of fear I can face and continue past. Only through dealing with our fears head on can we begin to overcome them and create new patterns that suit our desired outcome. Rather than run from fear, we must choose to run toward it. We must do what we're afraid of first and know that courage will come after.

FEAR – False Evidence Appearing Real

The presence of fear, like most emotions, can be traced back to the beginning of human history. Before we became such sophisticated animals, humans had as much, if not more, to fear in the wild than many other creatures out there, because frankly, we weren't all that scary. Our teeth aren't very sharp, we can't really run that fast, our nails and bones are brittle, and our skin is too bare to fight the cold and too thin to not be covered. If humans didn't end up banding together into groups and tribes, we stood little chance of ever surviving.

According to researchers, the first known human tribes are thought to have formed around 195,000 years ago. What's really interesting is that researchers also believe that humans didn't start speaking until about one hundred thousand years ago, which means for nearly half of our time in existence, humans communicated without words. No beautiful poetry, no late night heart-to-hearts, and no awkward conversations about the weather (though I think we can do without the latter).

By understanding how our ancestors lived, we can start to understand how fear may have played an important role in our development and perhaps how unimportant it may be today. For nearly the entire time we've been around, humans have lived in small tribes of no more than 100-150 people. These tribes offered safety and security through food, shelter, protection, and companionship. Members of the tribe had to live in cooperation with other members in order to ensure the integrity of the organization.

But as we know, not all tribe members cooperate. Some choose to go their own way or challenge authority. Some tribal members choose to hurt others and may threaten the safety of the group. In these instances, the strongest members of the tribe may decide to exile that member, sending them out into the wilderness to fend for themselves. Without adequate food, shelter, or protection from predators or the elements, it would become highly unlikely for them to survive.

It's believed by many ancient human history researchers that the modern day emotion of fear we experience is in fact an inherited instinctive emotion we've developed over thousands of years. This fear of being thrown out of our tribe is so deeply rooted in our psyche that humans experience it as an actual physical pain.

You might be thinking, "There are many fears other than rejection or death," but is that true? Hmm. I'll leave that one with you to ponder.

Although it is very possible for us to be rejected some way or another in this modern day and age, it's highly unlikely that we're going to be exiled out of society and left to fend off predators in the wild. For the most part, we have developed nourishing cultures throughout the world that offer a basis of living that we have deemed basic human rights. Still, humans in all societies and cultures suffer from this unrealistic fear. So much so that rather than face the possibility of rejection, many of us simply avoid socializing completely.

We live in a time where it's possible to connect with a loved one on the opposite side of the world through telephone, email, video calling, and much more. The theory of Six Degrees of Separation is moving closer to five or four, yet people still suffer from this widespread bashfulness. Some of us seem to be experiencing a fear of not being accepted, not being "good enough", and not being loved. But is this fear real, or is it simply a primitive programming we just need to understand and overcome?

Fear is an interesting emotion. It not only affects our mind but also has an immense effect on our physical state. When we experience fear, our body and mind shift into a primitive fight or flight response. This process has been passed on from our ancestors and is shared by almost every living thing. The fight or flight response is a physiological reaction to a *perceived* to be potentially harmful event or stimulus that *may* be a threat to our survival. The fight or flight response can also be understood as a very instinctive and primitive form of pattern matching.

In animals, including humans, this process involves a highly complex combination of chemical reactions, firing of neurons, and release of hormones that prime the animal for either fighting for survival or getting the hell out of town. The reaction starts in the amygdala, which triggers the hypothalamus and further on to the pituitary gland, which then leads to the release of steroidal hormones. While this is going on, the adrenal gland also gets excited and releases the neurotransmitter epinephrine, which then releases cortisol, the stress hormone.

All of these processes eventually increase muscle tension, blood pressure, and blood sugar in our bodies. The increased blood pressure sends glucose filled blood to our limbs, away from our internal organs. This preps the body for any intense physical efforts it may require such as running to safety or fighting for our lives. Unfortunately, because the majority of glucose filled blood has left our major organs, including the brain, our cognitive function may become limited.

Some other physical attributes of the fight or flight response include loss of hearing, tunnel vision, or loss of peripherals, shaking, accelerated breathing, and more. All of these reactions, though completely normal and intended for our survival, can clearly become overwhelming if occurring at inappropriate times or lasting for too long.

So why am I explaining all of this? Let's say you have that big presentation for the new job today. You're still scared to death of speaking, and you've done nothing to conquer it, but you decide that you have to at least try. You practice and practice, remembering everything you need to say, but when you get up in front of everyone, you freeze. Your body locks up, your heart starts pounding, and you completely forget everything you planned on presenting. It's like you've been stricken with amnesia. Your brain and other important organs have been stripped of their nutrients, leaving you in a nervous stupor, causing you to have a hard time remembering your name, let alone anything else.

After you leave the presentation with your tail between your legs, you reinforce the belief that you're terrible at speaking in front of people, that you'll fail if you try, and you go back to your old job thinking you're never going to change.

But we can change. We can take the steps **now** to get over our fears so that they don't take control when it matters most. We can take small steps toward dissecting our fears and beliefs so that we can take the power back in our lives. It might not be easy, and it's going to require courage, even if it's just a little bit at a time, but we can get there. It's been said that the opposite of love is not hate, but rather fear. Through overcoming these fears, we unlock the treasures of our own potential and allow ourselves to feel a deeper level of compassion, happiness, and love.

Believe it or not?

All right, so we understand where beliefs come from, how they form, and where they may or may not fit in our lives. We also have a good grasp on fear, where it comes from, and how it affects our bodies. Let's talk about what we can do about it.

When it comes to beliefs, it's not so easy to "un-believe" them. That's not really how the human mind works. It's like how once you figure out the answer to a riddle, you can't really un-know it. Beliefs, once formed, are usually there for life, unless you replace them.

Replacing beliefs can be achieved in a few steps. The first step is doing our best to understand what that belief is and where it came from. When was it formed? What happened in your life to create that belief, and in what ways have you reinforced it? It helps to write these things out. You may want to consider the help of professionals such as a counselor, psychologist, or even hypnotist to really get deep and figure it out, but you can definitely start on your own. Remember, there is absolutely no shame in asking others for help. We don't usually take our car to a plumber to get fixed; we take it to a mechanic. Our world is full of wonderful people who love what they do; give them the chance to live their dream while helping you achieve yours.

Once we have an idea of where the belief came from and how it formed, we have to start to disassemble it. If your belief is that every time you go on stage you'll fail, then start to really question that. Is it really true? What evidence do you have that supports it, and what evidence contradicts it? Are you selectively choosing which evidence you put your attention on? Author Byron Katie has written many books on the subject of removing limiting beliefs with her most popular being "The Work". In her book, she uses a technique that actually questions the legitimacy of your belief and helps you really take it apart and see it for what it is. Morty Lefko has also developed a great online program that helps you remove your limiting beliefs. I strongly suggest you look into these and other methods.

The final step is forming a new belief. As I mentioned earlier, it's not easy to "un-believe" something, but it is achievable to form a new belief. We're going to do so by finding an opposing belief to the one we're looking to remove. For example, if your belief is that you don't play music well, then perhaps part of forming a new belief will be to find an effective music teacher or to increase your practice time. Kevin Durant, NBA player, once said, "Hard work beats talent when talent doesn't work hard". There is no shortcut to success, and what seems like a failure now could be the very thing that leads you to the next step in achieving your dream. Facing this belief head-on will allow us to find opportunities to contradict it and form new, opposing beliefs. It might be a challenge, and it could get tough, but everything worth it always is.

Meditation for our Emotional Self

Meditation is often regarded as a cultivation of the mind. Pretty words, huh? Let me clarify. Before a farmer plants his seeds, he must prep the soil. Depending on what the soil was used for before will determine how much work there is to be done. If the area he's going to use was once a healthy garden, then the job won't be so much of a challenge. If the area used to be the parking lot of a power plant, then things might get a little tricky.

Our minds work the same way. Some of us have faced a life of hardships, abuse, and serious pain. This can leave a very dismal soil for planting new seeds of inspiration, motivation, and self-confidence. In order to prepare our minds for our highest potential, we have to cultivate the soil. Meditation can do just that. Meditation brings us to a state of acceptance and compassion, helping us remove doubt, fear, anger, resentment, insecurity, and more. Meditation can help release the traumas we've stored throughout our body and mind to make way for higher vibrations of love and peace.

Forgiveness

Forgiveness can be like that awkward hug the aunt you don't really know that well is trying to give you. You know that you should give it, but she always pinches your cheek and smells like strong perfume.

We have to give it, though, to others and ourselves. Holding grudges is like swallowing poison and expecting someone else to get sick. It creates dis-ease and disorder in our bodies and wreaks havoc on our emotional being. Holding grudges can subconsciously raise blood pressure and even increase the risk of heart disease. As expected, forgiving those people we have grudges against can relieve these conditions and even increase happiness and positivity.

Forgiving others is a gift to ourselves, maybe even more so than to those we are forgiving. Choosing love and peace allows us to vibrate at the frequency of those things we want—love and peace. From a higher perspective, forgiving others means that we have accepted that we are in control of our realities and the people and events we encounter. This doesn't mean we have to continue to be victimized or abused, but it does mean that we can let go of the anger and resentment we hold toward others.

When we forgive ourselves, we allow room for greater potential. On one hand, we can simply accept that there's nothing we can do to change the past and that our mistakes have lead us to where we are right now—a place of growth and readiness for change. On the other hand, depending on your beliefs, you might realize that everything you've ever been through, every moment you've ever experienced, has lead you perfectly and precisely to this moment right now. You have a gift deep inside you ready to come out when you're ready, but not a second before. The only question that remains is...are you ready?

Dealing With Others

When we start to get deep into creating our dream life, we may begin to wonder why there are still jerks out there. I mean, if I'm creating the environment around me, why am I creating rude waiters, aggressive drivers, and judgmental sales clerks? I'm not sure you're going to like the answers.

First of all, we have to ponder how these people might be of use in our lives. Once in a while when I'm writing a new blog, sharing a new recipe, or doing a seminar, I find myself dealing with skeptics. Some skeptics are highly educated and some are not. Sometimes they're respectful and offer a healthy debate, and sometimes they're downright rude. One thing they are consistently, though, is an inspiration. These people inspire me to double check my spelling, cross all my t's and dot all my i's. These people help me make sure that I cite my resources, offer accurate information, and present it clearly. I not only welcome skeptics, I'm truly grateful for them.

Then again, maybe the person cutting you off in traffic is triggering a chain of events that saves you from a car accident down the road. You'll never know, luckily, because they've cut you off. Maybe the rude waiter is need of love and is somehow sensing your strength and happiness while experiencing a little bit of jealousy or loneliness. Perhaps the judgmental sales clerk is actually just shy and feeling more judged by you than you are of her. There is always more to the story than we realize.

There's another trick I practice when a person is really giving me a challenge, and this might be the most important. I accept them. I accept them for who they are and let them be who they will be. While doing this, I imagine myself having a beautiful friendship with them, sharing inspiration and motivating each other. In my experience, when you accept someone for who they are, no matter how terrible they may be to you, one of two things will happen: they will either end up disappearing from your life, only coming and going a minimal amount of times at most, or eventually, they will at least become manageable. Part of shifting our realities is accepting things as they currently are. What we are experiencing in our lives now is a product of a previous intention. Some things, especially those that are deeply rooted within us, may take longer to change. The way we believe someone to be will determine who they will be. We can't expect someone to change as long as we believe them to be the opposite of what we want. We also can't expect to receive respect and acceptance for our ways if we don't offer it to others. We will cover these topics more in Vibratory Exchange and Quantum Delay, but in the meantime, try to give love, forgiveness, and acceptance as best you can. It's much easier to change how we perceive someone to be than it is to change them.

Additional Options

I'm a strong believer in supporting others and asking for support when I need it. As I mentioned earlier, there are people out there who are incredibly talented at their trade because it's their true calling in life. As an entrepreneur, a lot of the time, I find myself trying to cut corners here and there to save a few bucks, but that's the old school way of thinking. If our world is going to become the utopia paradise it has the potential to be, I believe we should all work together to employ each other to do what we love to do and help others in the process. Working on our emotional self is a great opportunity to do so.

There are incredible healers, counselors, coaches, and other passionate professionals whose lives are dedicated to helping people become better versions of themselves. I've sought out many of these types of people and have had incredible success. One of the first healers I worked with in my journey was a woman who was well versed in hypnosis as well as emotional freedom technique (EFT).

First of all, for those who have never had hypnosis performed, I urge you to keep an open mind. Some people are able to drop into a "hypnotic state", and others simply don't. I haven't had a trance-like experience *yet*, but now that I understand how hypnosis works, I know that's not required for success. As mentioned in The Now (at the end of the book), hypnosis is similar to guided meditation in that helps you get deep enough to plant suggestions into your subconscious mind. It can also be used to dig up old patterns that are buried deep in our psyche or even to try to remember our past lives. I found it a great tool for learning my old patterns, removing limiting beliefs, and overall healing. I know there will be some skeptics, but I urge you to at least try it out if it seems like something that resonates with you. You may have an incredible experience.

Emotional freedom technique or EFT (also known as "tapping") is a therapeutic method that uses a combination of acupuncture points on the body as well as positive affirmations to help remove deep, emotional traumas and blockages. Don't worry, there are no needles. The acupuncture points are simply tapped with a finger while the administrator says an affirmation that you repeat. An example might be, "even though my actions have hurt others, I still love and accept myself". It may sound a little bit elementary, but I assure you it works. There are thousands of well-known advocates, including Jack Canfield, author of Chicken Soup for the Soul.

Besides EFT and hypnosis, there are many other healing practices out there that all have great results including Reiki, psychology, re-connective healing, gonging, and much more. There is even a company called Biocybernaut that specializes in using a technology to manipulate a client's brain waves into reaching an almost "enlightened" state in very little time. The cost is extremely high ($10,000+) but similar results are attainable through meditation, self-exploration, and growth. The best bet is to get out and try a few to see which one gives you the best experience. It is well worth the effort.

Become Who You Are

An important thing to continue to remember in our growth is that we are not our thoughts, actions, or emotions, but rather something bigger than them all. We are something behind those thoughts and emotions, the "wizard behind the curtain", if you will. When you sit in silence and think of the first thought that comes to your mind, you'll often find yourself in a moment of nothingness. This is the mindfulness or presence we spoke about earlier, and that is the essence of whom you really are. All of the rest—the emotions, thoughts, stresses, worries—are all part of your mind, not your consciousness. They are not you, and you are not them.

When an old pattern or habit surfaces and bares its teeth, we can accept it and observe it as a manifestation of who we used to be. We will feel empowered in the observation of it because, through this observation and knowingness, we begin to elevate into our highest potential.

To build a foundation of a strong emotional self, we have to be willing to be honest with ourselves and dissolve the illusions we create. We have to let go of guilt and shame and accept who we are, both internally and externally. When we observe aspects of ourselves that we're not happy with, we must recognize them as reminders of our growth and not let them bring us down.

It's valuable to remember to go easy on ourselves and understand that this is all a process. The important thing is to continue to remind yourself what the future you would do. How would the future you react to situations? What type of composure and strength would that version of you have? It helps to write these ideas down and strive to become them. I don't believe in "fake it 'til you make it", but rather "believe it until you become it". We can change our self-expectations and create new patterns. Make it a goal to meet a new friend, change a belief, or conquer a fear each week. Talk to people in lines at the grocery store, take risks, and challenge yourself to grow and become more than you have been. You have the right to become your highest potential, and it all starts with a decision and intention to do so.

Shadow Work

Each of us has a dark side and aspects about our personality that we don't enjoy that serve as areas for improvement. This is inevitable and is part of the balance of our human experience. Through recognizing these parts of ourselves and working on improving the aspects, we can reach higher levels of our own potential while accepting who we are in the process. Facing fears, changing beliefs, having humility, and being honest with ourselves, among other personal development, are often referred to as *Shadow Work*. This work is as important, if not more, than any other aspects we can focus on while working on realizing our dreams. Shadow Work never ends and should be compared to maintenance on your vehicle or house cleaning. The more often you put energy and attention into it, the better things can be. Be sure to have plenty of patience and forgiveness for yourself while working on these traits, and remember the purpose is simply to recognize and transmute, not to make you feel worse.

My Practice

After the big break up and many nights of self-destruction, I realized there was some baggage that I needed to get rid of. I started with transcendental meditation, but I also experimented with hypnosis, EFT, Reiki, and psychology. These *all* proved to offer their own gifts and helped me clear out the weeds that were holding me back. In the end, I realized it all came down to overcoming the fear of facing my own shortcomings. Once we know something about ourselves, it's hard to turn a blind eye. Ignorance may seem like bliss, but the subconscious patterns we've created over the years can really hold us back, and the first step is awareness of their existence.

Homework

Curious Creator – any 3   Master Manifestor – all

1) **Be honest with yourself.** What are your three biggest areas for improvement (ex. temper, impatience, selfishness, greed)? What have they held you back from creating? Name one step for how you will improve each.

2) **Get a tune-up.** Everyone could use a tune-up and a bit of de-stressing. Consult and receive treatment in any of the following: massage, Reiki, acupuncture, EFT, hypnosis, counseling, reflexology, and/or group meditation.

3) **Be courageous.** What are your three biggest fears? What have they held you back from? Name one way you will begin to overcome each.

4) **Forgive.** Who is one person in your life who you should forgive? Find this person and make amends. Be patient with them and yourself.

5) **Meditate.** Meditation is the most valuable tool in manifestation. It helps remove limiting beliefs and fears

that no longer serve us and allows us to shift in alignment with our desires. For best results, make time to meditate every day.

6) **Journal.** It doesn't need to be anything special, just write a paragraph or two about how your day was. There are lots of daily journal websites out there. You can find my favorite at www.rickygoodall.com

"The doctor of the future will no longer treat the human frame with drugs, but rather will cure and prevent disease with nutrition."

-Thomas Edison

"Those who think they have no time for exercise will sooner or later have to find time for illness."

-Edward Stanley

ELEMENT 2

PHYSICAL SELF

Though I've written the Emotional Self and Physical Self as separate chapters, it could be understood that together, they make up the full *human* self. They could also be understood as the mind-body construct or the total entity that comprises of the psychological and physiological being each of us experiences life through. Our physical self is composed of our living body, the processes within it, and how we use it. This also includes the chemical reactions within our brain, which of course bleeds into the emotional aspect of our construct. Try to visualize the physical self as an extension of our emotional being. The two aspects together, along with our inner essence, are often referred to as the manifestation of mind, body, and soul.

I'm going to be covering a few different topics that may resonate well with some people and not so well with others. As with all of the information in this book, I invite you to take what is currently working for you and disregard what you don't need. Despite what you're willing to accept in this moment, try to at least entertain some of these ideas, and if you feel the desire, put some research into them yourself. I assure you that anything I put in ink has at least been researched to the point where I feel comfortable sharing it with others. Of course, theories change, and new information will become available, potentially trumping some of the things I'll be speaking about, but that's ok. I welcome change and am an avid practitioner of humility.

As a nutrition coach, I have to be on top of my game when it comes to relevant and recent research. I have to be sure that the theories I'm using for my clients and I are up-to-date and accurate. In saying that, sometimes the "best" information is not the best fit for a client's goals, lifestyle, or preferences. Being a good coach means a balance of efficient methodology paired with effective execution. In other words, I need to make sure I'm using a balance of the best techniques in a way my client can utilize them and keep consistent. There's no point in putting a client on a plan that they are going to simply give up on a week in because it's too intimidating. My job is to make sure I'm creating a plan that matches their current place in life while also challenging them to reach a higher level of potential. When reading the aspects in this chapter, as well as all of the others, I invite you again to choose to practice ideas that match your current lifestyle while challenging yourself to push a little bit further and step a bit outside your comfort zone. This is where exponential growth will occur.

Our Body is Our Temple

The way we treat our body is vital to the experience we're going to have throughout our life. The things we put in our body and how we treat it will have a significant impact on the thought processing, energetic output, and vibratory exchange we give out to the world. We may get so caught up in our emotions and ego that we neglect our physical bodies. It's important to be mindful of how we treat it because we only get one, at least in this lifetime.

It's often said that a clean house is a clean mind, and the same thing can be said about our bodies; they truly are our temples. A body that works efficiently and healthily will ensure a full, enjoyable experience. This doesn't mean that vacations, fun meals, or a bit of downtime isn't suggested. It means that we should practice an idea of all things in moderation with a focus on alignment with our highest purpose.

An Old View on Newtrition

As we move deep into the information age and research is available at our finger tips, it's becoming clear and apparent that the food we put into our bodies is more than just "calories in, calories out". For those unfamiliar with this term, it means that according to older, outdated interpretations, the food we put into our body can be calculated easily by the calories it provides versus the calories expended in daily activity. That would mean that if we ate a one-hundred calorie cupcake, we would just have to do one hundred calories worth of exercise to "burn it off". Unfortunately, it's not that simple.

There are many other processes that occur in our bodies that determine how food is utilized, including chemical reactions, hormone communication, and much more. Eating one hundred calories from bread is not the same as eating one hundred calories from rice. The way that food is used in our body is much different and depends on many other factors.

Many other research findings have also suggested there is much more to our food than even the nutrients we can easily measure. Some research has been showing us that the source of our food has a huge effect on the bioavailability of nutrients and how well our body can use the nutrients present. The types of food we eat also have a major impact on our mood, energy levels, and much more.

Though I feel I could fill an entire book with nutrition information, I'm going to stick to a few specific points to take into consideration. Again, the points I highlight here are based on the most current information, and as more information becomes available, these points may become more or less apparent and supported.

The important point to take is that the foods we eat truly affect how we feel and live our lives. Important hormones, such as dopamine and serotonin, regulate our mood and are heavily influenced by the foods we put into our bodies. The foods we eat can lead to seemingly endless energy or a zombie-like mid afternoon crash that even caffeine can't fix. What we put in can truly determine what we put out.

Who Let The Dogmas Out?

It seems as more information becomes available, there are more and more "perfect" diets out there. Last week, it might have been Atkins, this week, Paleo, and next week, Vegan. The battle to be an advocate of the best diet has become the ultimate pissing contest. Many people are more concerned about the illusion of "best" versus the reality of "best for me". The truth is it's highly unlikely that we'll ever find out what the "best" eating style is, and the definition of such comes in the qualification process. As you'll see in the information ahead, there are some very important points to consider when making choices for an eating style. If your decision is influenced by the most humane and close to natural style, then you may gravitate toward Paleo, Warrior Diet, or Raw eating. If your decision is based on less impact in animal consumption, you may move toward veganism or vegetarianism. Then again, if your decision is based on aesthetics alone, you may choose another direction. There are a lot of decisions that can influence an eating style, and the important thing to always remember is to listen to your intuition and follow your heart. What works for someone else may not work for you, and what works for you may not work for others. It's very important, when looking to live our dreams, that we respect the decisions of others and what resonates with them and find what resonates with us. All too often, someone will become very enthusiastic and passionate about a cause that hits home for them, and they create a dogma from it. Choice is a very important part of creation, and everyone has the right to make their own.

When I'm asked questions like "which eating style is best?" and "do humans need to eat meat?" I like to answer it like this: The eating style that is best is the one that is in alignment with the person you wish to be. It's the style of eating that you feel in your heart is best for you, and if you don't know, then perhaps you should find a professional who can help educate you to make the right decision. If you feel that eating animals is cruel, then you should seek someone who can help you transition into an appropriate vegan or vegetarian diet. If you're someone who wants to eat meat but sees everything wrong with the mainstream food industry, then you should start shopping locally and buying your food from farmers you trust. Though humans can become very healthy from a meat-containing *or* meat-free diet, the choice must remain up to the individual. Despite popular belief, there are not as many vegan animals in nature as we might assume. Cows eat grass, but within that grass often come worms and other bugs. When you take the cow out of the pasture and supplement its protein intake with grains and soy, it becomes sick.

We all have an incredible guidance system sitting between our ears and inside our chest. Listen closely, and you'll find all of the answers you need.

A Bone to Pick

The curtain has started to fall on the food industry with consumers becoming much more aware of what they're eating. We're starting to realize that it's not just what you eat, but it's where it came from, how it was raised or grown, and the processing that takes place in between. What happens between the farm and your plate is a big deal.

Let's take animal products, for example. Humans have been eating cattle for about ten thousand years. When beef was first introduced to the Americas in the 1400s, cows started being raised on farms, eating grass from their pasture. For hundreds of years, North Americans ate beef without any significantly related medical issues. In the 1970s, during the industrial revolution, the food industry started taking a dark turn. Animals such as cows, pigs, chickens, and others were being taken off the farm and thrown into Concentrated Animal Feeding Operations, or CAFO's. These operations were modeled after a production line not unlike the ones you see in car or toy factories. These CAFO's hold anywhere from one hundred to one thousand animals in highly unsanitary and inhumane conditions. The environmental impact alone is enough to make a person cringe. CAFO's generate millions of tonnes of manure every year, which presents a risk to local water quality and creates enormous amounts of pathogens. They release several types of gas emissions, such as ammonia, hydrogen sulfide, methane, and more, all of which have significant human health risks.

These operations also partake in questionable bioengineering practices such as the administration of   recombinant bovine growth hormone (rbGH) to promote milk production, as well as estrogen, testosterone, and progesterone to speed up growth and production. Antibiotics are also administered to treat infections caused by the unsanitary feedlot conditions and improper feed. All of these drugs may be absorbed by humans through ingestion of the meat and cause increased risks of diseases such as cancer and tolerance of important antibiotic medication.

In CAFO's, cattle are often fed a diet high in grains and soy versus grass, their natural food source. This causes severe digestive issues in the animal, and in some cases instant death. When the animal becomes infected from the food, it must be administered antibiotics for treatment. Cows are sometimes labeled as "hormone free" or "organic" but are still fed grain as their primary food source. This simply means that the animal could be facing the *same* medical issues as the hormone-administered cows except they don't receive any treatment. This is not good.

Besides the inhumane conditions the animal suffers, there is also a huge impact on their nutrients in the meat itself. Beef from cows that are fed grass will contain important nutrients such as conjugated linoleic acid (CLA), Omega 3, stearic acid, a healthy saturated fatty acid, Vitamin K2, and much more. All of these nutrients are extremely beneficial to our health and can actually help lower the risk of heart disease, high blood pressure, cancer, and many other medical issues. Beef from grain fed cows, such as those raised in CAFO's, contains nearly none of these nutrients, yet a higher ratio of the unhealthy saturated fats and cholesterol. Besides the lack of nutrients, this beef may also contain remnants from the drugs administered as well as trace amounts of feces and other stomach-turning organisms.

Other animals such as chickens, pig, and many others are treated this way. This means the beef in your restaurant hamburgers, chicken at your grocery store, or hot dogs at the baseball game most likely contain meat from a CAFO-raised animal unless clearly indicating otherwise.

When shopping for animal products, make sure you know where you're buying from. Shopping at local butchers, farmer's markets, or even directly from the farm gives you the option to ask where the meat has come from, how the animals were raised, and what they were fed. The people selling the products are often very friendly and eager to talk about how humanely the animal was raised.

Lettuce talk Organic for a Minute

Organic, Certified Organic, Organically Grown, Locally Grown, Locally and Organically Grown... What does it all mean? Does it even matter?

Organic food is food that is produced in a way that complies with standards set by an official governing body. Organic food *should* be free of synthetic chemicals and pesticides. Some organic food may contain pesticides, but those pesticides must come from natural sources such as certain types of plants. Other foods may be grown organically, meaning without the use of chemicals or pesticides but aren't *certified* organic. There can be many reasons for this, one as simple as the farmer not being able to afford to or choosing not to have his products officially certified. This doesn't always mean that they are any less healthy than a certified food; in fact, in some cases they may even be healthier.

Synthetic pesticides have been linked to lots of health issues such as cancer, Alzheimer's disease, ADHD, birth defects, and much more. They potentially harm the nervous system, endocrine system, and reproductive system. A single berry can contain up to 30 different types of chemicals.

In terms of how likely it is that the pesticides will affect you, most inorganic food will fall into one of two categories. These categories have been deemed the "dirty dozen" and the "clean fifteen". The dirty dozen are foods like apples, berries, and others that may not have a tough exterior protecting the insides from contamination or other qualities that make them easily exposed. The clean fifteen includes foods like avocado and grapefruit. A simple Google search will offer a more detailed description and food list. This list can change, so it's a good idea to stay up-to-date as best as possible.

Lighten Up

There's another important quality of food that is only beginning to surface around the world. Researchers have begun to put focus on an aspect of plants and some animal products called *biophotons*. Biophotons are biological light particles found in every living thing in nature, and until the last few years were basically overlooked—but not for long.

Our bodies also contain biophotons, and according to researchers such as Dr. Fritz-Albert Popp, they're a pretty big deal. He suggests that the cells in our body communicate in a coherent light field relying on biophotons. They can lower the state of entropy, or disorder in a living body. This means that a body high in biophotons would be less chaotic and have a much higher level of cellular communication. While our cells use about one hundred thousand chemical reactions per cell per second, only a small amount of biophotons is needed because of this coherent light field. German author Marco Bishcof writes in his book *Biophotons - The Light in Our Cells*, "All living cells of plants, animals, and human beings emit biophotons, which cannot be seen by the naked eye but can be measured by special equipment developed by German researchers."

According to Dr. Popp, cancer cells will actually "suck in" biophotons, robbing the surrounding cells of their luminescence. This will in turn cause disorder and chaos, decreasing the body's cells' ability to communicate efficiently. Poor communication can lead to decreased recovery and increased illness. If a biophoton measurement is taken for a patient who is vibrantly healthy, they will light up like a Christmas tree, whereas if the patient is suffering from an illness, they won't.

Interestingly enough, raw, close to fresh foods are loaded with biophotons, with wild foods having the highest concentration. Free-range hens' eggs are also known to have a high biophoton count, with caged hen's eggs having nearly none. Plants emit ten thousand biophotons per second while humans emit about eight to ten per second.

Plants will have the highest concentration of biophotons right after they're picked with the amount decreasing more as time passes. Fruits or vegetables at a grocery store, organic or inorganic, will contain significantly less biophotons because of the time it takes from farm to shelf. Cooking food will also destroy them.

So you might be wondering, what does this all mean and what's the point? There are some studies that suggest that eating a food containing raw, organic fruits and vegetables shows substantial benefits, but the reason why is confusing. For a while, people were jumping on the live enzyme bandwagon, but recent research suggests that live enzymes may not survive our stomach acid. Plant enzymes have a much broader pH range, suggesting that they can survive the acidity of our stomach, but more research is needed to confirm that. There is ample research showing the benefits of biophotons, however.

Many serious illnesses such as cancer and diabetes have been treated and even reversed using a raw plant-based diet. Humans have been using plants for thousands of years to treat ailments and still do today. Some studies even show that walking outside in bare feet can increase biophoton counts in our body. This technique is called *grounding* or *earthing* and has also been used for tens of thousands of years. Researchers have discovered that meditation has been shown to slow the "leaking" of biophotons in test subjects. Practitioners of Qigong, Reiki, and other healing practices are beginning to attribute aspects their techniques to the manipulation and direction of biophoton energy. Some advocates suggest that biophotons may even be a physical manifestation of *Prana*, or our life force, though such claims might be deemed simply optimistic. One thing we know for sure is that every living thing shares and contains this light energy.

I'm going to step outside of the scientific reasoning for a second and suggest something. Would it be all that crazy to think that perhaps local, organic, or wild food eaten in its most natural state and still containing energy from the sun (light energy AKA biophotons) might actually have substantial health benefits? Would it be completely nuts to suggest that maybe our planet provides everything we need and that some things are beyond our total understanding even now? Hmm...

I'm not suggesting that anyone completely transition to a total raw, plant-based diet—unless it is something they desire—but I think there is more than enough reason to believe incorporating at least some of these foods into a lifestyle can have some big health benefits.

I spent a fair amount of time on the nutrition aspect of this chapter for a few reasons. First of all, it's one of my big passions, and a lot of my life has been dedicated to understanding it as best I can with intention to change my own life and the lives of others. Secondly, I know that it can be one of the most confusing subjects out there. Society has created a taboo with nutrition, playing on the heart strings of those sitting in the dark wondering where to go next. Though my suggestion is always to either do your own research or seek out the help of a professional whose passion is nutrition and helping others, I'll also close this portion with a few simple tips for working toward your own healthy nutrition:

If it comes in a package or is heavily processed, avoid it. If it has been treated poorly or has been maximized for profit, avoid it. If it has an expiration date that will outlast the lifetime of a house plant, avoid it. Follow your heart and work toward the best practices for your own alignment.

Beyond The Kitchen

Although nutrition is a huge precursor to health, happiness, and longevity, what we do with our bodies is also very important. As technology advances, we're finding people working jobs with much less physical activity. Factory workers, labourers, and many other jobs are being lost to machines, and people are turning to office jobs and ultimately spending hours every day working in front of a computer. Because of this, it's important that we supplement our lives with exercise and other physical activities.

Staying active isn't just to keep our bodies in top shape, either. In fact, exercise can work wonders on our emotional self, as well. Low to moderate amounts of exercise have been shown to reduce depression, reduce stress, increase self-esteem, and much more. Though there are many types of ways to exercise, something as little as a daily walk or a low impact exercise class can influence these positive effects.

Meditation in Motion

Some great ways to incorporate mindfulness and exercise together are through yoga, dance, martial arts, and sex. Each of these activities can access parts of our mind that will take us away from the daily stresses in our lives and keep us anchored in the moment. Through focusing on our body's movements and/or the movements of others, we can send our fears, worries, and stresses away and be present in the now.

Participating in an exercise class can help keep your workout interesting. It also helps to have someone else keep you accountable and take the lead. Participating in a martial arts class, fitness class, or even working with a personal trainer can keep things interesting and help you achieve goals you may not have realized you could achieve. Most exercise classes and clubs offer the first class free so you can try a few out and see which ones work for you.

Be Like Water

Medical professionals say our bodies are made up of 75 percent water. That means that every movement you make, every thought you think, and every stimulus you experience is only possible because of the water in your body. It can't be stressed enough how important it is to take in high quality water every day. Dehydration is one of the most common causes of headaches, depression, muscle fatigue, and many other serious health issues. An active adult can divide their weight by fifty and calculate how many litres of water they should drink *every* day. This should be outside of the coffee, teas or other beverages you may be drinking.

The water you drink shouldn't be just any water, though. Tap water and even many types of bottled water contain very harmful contaminants such as chlorine and fluoride which can be detrimental to our health.

Contrary to popular belief, fluoride is incredibly toxic and should not be consumed. Many countries across the globe have completely banned fluoride from their drinking water. There are numerous studies that suggest that fluoride may lower IQ, cause brain damage, impede thyroid function, cause arthritic symptoms, damage bones, and even calcify the pineal gland.

One Gland to Rule Them All

The pineal gland is one of the most mysterious and misunderstood parts of our brain. This gland is shaped like a pine cone and actually contains rods and cones, just like our eyes. Many religions call it our "third eye" or "mind's eye", and Egypt's "Eye of Horus" looks just like the side view of the pineal gland. The pine cone symbol has been seen in many religions including Christianity, Catholicism, Hinduism, Buddhism, and others. René Descartes, an avid studier of the pineal gland, called it the "principal seat of the soul".

The pineal gland produces melatonin, which is responsible for our circadian rhythm and is believed to produce a very peculiar chemical called Dimethyltryptamine or DMT. This chemical is believed to assist in helping produce our dream experiences as well as the visions we see in near death experiences. It's potentially found in almost every living thing and has been extracted from plants for thousands of years to be used as one of the most powerful psychedelic medicines on Earth. There have been many documentaries about this chemical, including the most popular, *"DMT: The Spirit Molecule"*. This documentary explores the affects of the compound on many subjects in a controlled setting. Nearly every subject claimed an intense and euphoric spiritual experience which has changed their lives forever.

Tribes all over the world, including places like Tibet and Peru, hold ceremonies using this chemical to lead others into a spiritual journey. What significance could the most powerful psychedelic compound in the world have in our bodies? Why have countless religions and tribes associated the pineal gland to being a spiritually significant part of our mind?

It is said that between 60-80 percent of Europeans and North Americans have a partially or completely calcified pineal gland. When a pineal gland is calcified, it cannot work the way it's designed to, including the release of melatonin and DMT when necessary, among many other issues. Calcification can happen in many ways, including eating processed foods, abusing alcohol, cigarettes, and other drugs, drinking fluoridated water, and more.

A calcified pineal gland is associated with weight gain and obesity, slow thyroid function, poor circulation, poor mood, mental disorders, lack of vision, lower IQ, and many other serious issues. When the pineal gland is decalcified, a person will experience vivid and lucid dreams, improved sleep, enhanced imagination, improved sexual function, and much more.

Luckily, we can work toward decalcifying our pineal gland in our everyday lives. The first step is to avoid further calcification through drinking fluoride-filtered tap water and avoiding excessive use of drugs and alcohol, and limiting our ingestion of processed and inorganic foods. Some foods and supplements will help, such as MSM, raw cacao, garlic, Vitamin K1/K2, melatonin, boron, chaga mushroom, and organic fruits and vegetables. Regular exercise, yoga, and meditation will also help decalcify the pineal gland. There is a fantastic company in Canada called Conscious Water who carries fluoride filters and offers many other products that can help with this process. You can visit them at www.consciouswater.ca

Like many topics in this book, I could write chapters upon chapters about the pineal gland, but I strongly urge you to work toward decalcification the best you can. It will improve your overall health and happiness and will increase your ability to imagine and manifest your dreams.

Maintain Your Vehicle

In today's day and age, it's easy to get distracted by the meetings, deadlines, bills, and television, but we truly have to treat our bodies with the respect they deserve. A healthy body will yield a healthy mind, and what's the point of creating a magical dream life if we're not going to be here long enough to enjoy it? This doesn't mean you have to work toward looking like a cover model or elite athlete, but it does mean that you need to spend some time getting up and moving around every day, no matter how simple the activity. Take a walk outside; take the stairs instead of the elevator, and park a little bit further away in the parking lot. Stand up for a couple minutes for every half hour you spend sitting down.

We can think of our bodies as either being a swamp or a river. The water in a swamp becomes stale and old, with nothing new moving through it, whereas a river is continually pulsing with life, changing with every moment. We have to treat our bodies better than we'd treat a brand new vehicle. If we do, we'll get to enjoy them well into the Golden Years.

My Practice

Issues with eating and weight were a challenge for me for most of my life with my heaviest weight being 250 pounds. When I began my MMA career, I really started to understand the importance of my nutrition. Eating for health rather than for momentary satisfaction not only helped me drop seventy-five pounds, but it also added to my self-esteem, happiness, health, and well-being. The clarity, calmness, and overall increased energy we can harness from eating properly not only changes our body composition but our entire outlook on life.

Every day, I have a fresh serving of raw, organic vegetables, and all of my meats (about one serving per day) are locally and humanely raised. I have one or two Victory Meals‡ per week, and drink three or four litres of fluoride-free, filtered water per day. I use super foods and natural supplements and avoid anything processed. Taking it one step at a time and reminding ourselves why this is important to us can work wonders. I get my clients to write down five reasons they're working on their nutrition and keep it in their pocket. When they're feeling challenged, they can read them to themselves and remember why they're doing it in the first place. We all deserve to become a higher version of our own potential.

I have not transitioned to a completely animal-free diet in my life, though I do feel an intuitive desire to at minimize my intake of animal product. Rather than call my eating style *vegan* or *vegetarian* I simply call it "plant-based."

Besides the changes in nutrition, I also make sure I exercise at least sixty minutes every day. For me, that can mean martial arts, running, weight training or yoga. As I mentioned earlier, yoga, martial arts and dance are great ways to practice mindfulness and exercise at the same time. You can practice at home or in a class; both are great.

‡A Victory Meal is a meal consumed 1-2 times per week that can be any meal you like. This meal serves as an emotional reward for all of the hard work of eating clean and strict as well as a physiological tool to increase metabolism and enhance the body's ability to expel toxins.

Homework

Curious Creator – any 3   Master Manifestor – all

1) **Move it.** Participate in any type of motivating exercise activity (ex. spin class, TRX, Crossfit, running group, personal training session, or anything where someone else leads you). Make friends. If you check out www.elevatedwellness.org, we have lots of classes that might inspire you.

2) **Clean up.** Participate in a cleanse (2-30 days long, your choice). See it through to the end. Journal how you feel during.

3) **Meditate in motion.** Participate in any one (or all) of the following: martial arts class, yoga class, dance class,

or even weight lifting (put your mind in your muscle).

4) **Drink clean.** Get a fluoride water filter. If you're in Canada, you can find them at www.consciouswater.ca. You will thank me later.

5) **Lighten up.** Strive to eat at least one or two servings of raw, organic food everyday to get a healthy dose of biophotons.

6) **Respect your food.** If you're going to eat meat, please eat humanely raised meat. If you're in a circumstance where you have no choice, then so be it, but spend your money wisely. You're voting with your dollars.

7) **Eat better.** If you eat well now, then that's great. If not, do your best to make changes. If you're not sure which changes to make, there are endless professionals who can help you. We have lots of great coaches who can coach you online through www.thenutritionblueprint.com and www.elevatedwellness.org.

8) **Go outside.** Do it every day, and if it's nice enough outside, do it barefoot. Trust me!

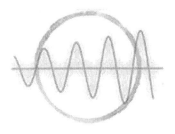

"Giving opens the way for receiving."

-Florence Scovel Shinn

ELEMENT 3

VIBRATORY EXCHANGE

In this chapter, we start getting into some really fun stuff. When brainstorming this book, I decided to leave out any words like "law" or "rule" because for those of you who read The Underworld later in the book, you'll see that *laws* are not always what they seem. If I was going to propose any of my concepts to be considered a law, it might be called "The Law of Vibratory Exchange". In short, this law might be described as something along the lines of "what you put out, you get back; therefore, what you get back, you must put out."

I want to start by explaining an important concept. When it comes to creating our dreams—no matter how big or small—it's important to understand what our ultimate intention is. We should try to remember what each of these dreams represent and what state of mind we're looking to experience through actualizing them: happiness. Now, I say the state we're looking to experience rather than the state we're looking to achieve because happiness is not some place or something we get to or some *thing* we create. Happiness is a state that is continually experienced through the journey itself. It's important for us to find joy in the act of *creating* the dream as much as settling into the dream itself. The nervousness, the wonder, the stress—it is all part of the journey. That exhilaration we get when we're close to the finish line is something that can be experienced continually as long as we remember this principle.

The confusion for some people comes in the difference between satisfaction and happiness. If The Wright Brothers were always satisfied, they likely would have never created the airplane. If Mark Zuckerberg was always satisfied, he would have never created Facebook. If it weren't for dissatisfaction, we would probably still be living in caves using rocks for tools. It's ok, and in fact encouraged, to be dissatisfied with something or many things, but that doesn't mean we can't find happiness in that dissatisfaction. Through practicing gratitude, allowing ourselves to "settle into the dream" and be present in the moment, we can experience a level of bliss and happiness second to none. It's easy to get caught up in the hustle and bustle of the dream, but taking time to ground ourselves and see where we've come can really help us find happiness in the dissatisfaction.

Good Vibrations

The vibrations we send out into the universe have a major impact on the reality we experience. Our thoughts, words, feelings, and choices quite literally shape the world around us. This can be a scary thought for many people, but for me, it's incredibly exciting. If we can learn how to harness and utilize this concept, then we can—and will—change our lives forever.

It can be an overwhelming experience. Knowing that everything you think, say, and do can potentially bring you both enjoyable experiences and extremely uncomfortable ones can be enough to make a person go crazy. Learning to be accountable for the vibrations you put out is similar to learning a new language; it's going to be frustrating and upsetting sometimes. But I assure you, if you put in the work and trust the process, the outcome will be nothing short of your wildest dreams.

When I first started learning these ideas, I had the expected resistance. Most days, I'd wonder if I was crazy. Other days, I'd be so stricken with fear or nervousness that I'd almost give up on the ideas completely. But luckily for me, and hopefully you, I pushed through and found my rhythm.

This chapter is going to cover some of the real reasons we're all here. It's going to help you increase the abundance in your life. It's going to help you find love. It's going to help you have a better social life, a better career, and a better overall happiness. If utilized, the tools in this chapter could change everything you thought about your life and the world around you.

The concepts here will start to show results in your life immediately. They might be small and incremental in the beginning, but they will shortly move up to bigger experiences. Depending on your resistance, fears, and limiting beliefs, it may take a bit longer. Because of this, I'm asking you to stay consistent and driven for at least **fourteen days.** We're going to cover the concept of Quantum Delay later on, but in summary, it takes time for the universe to respond to your vibrations, and it won't work on your time. It takes patience and belief before things manifest, and people often give up right before a big change is going to happen.

When we plant a seed into soil, we walk away and trust that it will sprout. We don't nervously come back a couple of times a day, dig it up, and see if it's sprouting yet; if we did, it would die. We plant the seed knowing and trusting that nature will do its job and bring us growth. "What you sow, so shall you reap" is not a phrase limited to farmers. This is a proverb that can be used to explain all of nature and the entirety of Vibratory Exchange.

A Bun Dance

The term "abundance" has been thrown around a lot in the past few years, especially since the movie The Secret. Everyone wants it! There are tonnes of affirmations (we'll get to them) out there about it. "I easily and gracefully manifest abundance into my life." "Abundance flows to me easily and effortlessly."

Once, I had a listener at one of my presentations come up to me and ask, "What sort of affirmations do you use to attract abundance? I've been using a few, and they don't seem to be working."

I was curious, so I asked, "First, how about you tell me what abundance is to you?"

To which she responded, "Isn't it money?"

Isn't it? Not exactly. Well, maybe sometimes. Let me elaborate.

Abundance might be better understood as energy. Money

however can be understood better as something material. The confusion lies in the definition of money. Money is a symbolic representative of whatever it is we can get for it, but it is not the thing we desire. If a vacation is what you desire you might say, "I need money so I can go", but I challenge that statement. Do you really need money to go on a vacation? Perhaps you could win an all expenses paid trip or have a friend take you for free. You might need a passport, a plane, and some dorky shorts but actual money is debatable.

Money vs. Abundance

I won't lie, I enjoy money. I don't love it, and I know I don't *need* it, but I do enjoy it. I think a perfect world will be a balance of money and abundance together.

While realizing our dreams, it's important to remain detached from *how* our dream will manifest. For example, if your dream is to manifest a beautiful car, then that car could come in two possible ways: with money, or without it. Now, you might be thinking, "I thought you said we don't need money". I do stand by that. However, I also mentioned that money can be used as a tool. So while manifesting your dreams, you might find yourself with an abundance of opportunities to make more money than you usually do. This may *also* be your opportunity to go out and get yourself that dream car or to start putting some money away for the down payment. The universe might be providing you with the *lifestyle* of the person you will be when you own that car, so you need to align your life with it accordingly. The car will require insurance, maintenance, and other expenses, so the universe is probably prepping you for that before you get it by offering financial opportunities. It's important to recognize them and start to shift into the person you will be when you manifest your dream.

Sometimes our dreams will come without the need for money, and other times, they come in the form of opportunities that inevitably lead to them. Be sure to recognize the difference between abundance and money, and you will open the doors of possibility for your desires to manifest.

Become a Word Smith

I'm a huge fan of words, but they can be a little funny. You can say something two different ways, and by definition, it may come off almost exactly the same. An example might be when you're asked, "How are you?" One common response could be "Good". Another could be "Not bad". By definition, "not bad" might be understood as "good", but is not bad really good? Where do you make the differentiation? Does it matter? I think it does.

The universe is tricky; it almost acts a bit autistic. When you say "good", your environment will respond with "good" situations. But when you say "not bad", it just hears "bad" and responds accordingly.

The words we use are important, they say a lot more than we might realize. I have a friend who continually says he's broke. He might get a raise at work or come into some money somehow, but his default status is "broke". This is a problem.

When you tell the story of "being broke", then the reality you're going to experience is going to be one of "being broke". I know, I know... Sometimes you feel like you have to choose between feeding the kids and buying new shoes, but in those cases, you can empower yourself and say, "I'm choosing to save my money today" or "I'd rather not spend money on that". Being "broke" is a victim mentality where making choices is something the empowered do. We should always keep the frame of mind that the place we find ourselves in right *now* is a product of the vibrations we put out *before.* Unless we want to continue experiencing what we're experiencing right now, then we had better change the story we're telling.

V is for Vent-etta

Venting can be a slippery slope. We get so worked up that we just need to get something off our chests to someone, and before we know it, we're stuck in a negative feedback loop, feeding off of each other's misery. It's very important to avoid this practice. In times where we feel we just really need to get something out, we should already have an agreement with a member of our Dream Team—people that know to listen then use positive redirection to get us back on course. Venting can be healthy and productive if it leads to a solution, but getting stuck on the problem can only lead to more problems. If a problem exists, then it is creating contrast for you to know what it is you do desire. Use that contrast to help find the solution and start telling the story you *do* want to hear.

Create a Dream Team

Once in a while we get into a great flow of good vibrations, but then the world around us comes back into our focus. All of the gossip, reality TV, morbid news, and much more floods into our lives. Conspiracy theories, economic downturn, potential layoffs. We end up absorbing this information, automatically regurgitating it back to our friends and family, and before we know it, we're falling back into old patterns. A great way to avoid this slippery slope is to create what I like to call a "Dream Team". Get a group of people together, whether it's one or one hundred, and make pact to keep each other accountable in your words and thoughts. Have an agreement that when one starts to go on a negative path that the other one will hear them out then give a positive redirection. Some great ways to do this would be to ask, "What are you excited for right now?" or "What are you grateful for today?" It's nearly impossible to answer these questions and stay in a counterproductive mind space. If the subject feels too pressing to move on from, then perhaps the question could be, "What are we going to do about it?" Having a Dream Team to keep you accountable can help you move mountains. It's believed that we are the average of the five people we spend the most time with. Who are you spending yours with?

The Fear Agenda

This is the only time you're going to hear me address this topic because, in my reality, it doesn't exist. I hope you'll create your reality in the same way, but for now, this might help. I know there are problems in the world. Be it the economy, the government, the wars... I know, it's terrible; but that's not the world I want to live in, so I'm not going to tell that story. The world we live in *today* is a product of our thoughts, words, and choices *yesterday*. I want to live in a world of happiness, peace, and abundance for all. That world exists inside of me, and I'm doing my best to manifest it into the world around me through my thoughts, my words, and my actions.

Nearly every economic downfall results in the largest entrepreneurial revolution until that time. When people are forced out of the jobs they don't really like anyway, they're given the opportunity to chase the dream they thought may have died long ago. I know that some people aren't so lucky, and my heart goes out to them, but the most valuable growth is often painful.

The people responsible for these world problems are also people, just like you and I. That may be hard to believe—I have a hard time with it too—but if we can believe that *we* can change, then we *must* allow them the same respect. If there is a fear agenda, then the power lies in our fear and our ignorance. I think it's safe to say that we're no longer ignorant to the world's problems, but many of us have transmuted that awareness into a deeper fear. This fear still keeps us trapped. If you want to see a better world, then start in your own community by helping those you know and those you don't. When a friend or colleague brings you a story of the world we've created in our past, use the same positive redirection you'd use for any negativity. How can we change it? What can we do now? How can we take some responsibility and make it better? Don't accept complacency as an answer; there are options and there are ways to fix it. Find what works for you, and get to it.

We're doing well. We're living in the best time in our history, despite how it may seem. The main stream media likes to focus on the bad, but as futurist, Jason Silva, points out, "The number of men dying at the hands of *other men* is the least it's ever been in history." What story do you want to hear?

SIDENOTE: I admit, there's a system that exists in some developed countries that is intended to create factory workers from the time of an early age. Our high school and post-secondary education system was basically designed to train people to prepare for a corporate life working for others. It wasn't created to promote creativity and opportunity primarily. Even the student loan program sets students up for years of debt after graduation. This system does still exist, but there is a new system forming that offers a choice. There is a system of community gaining strength that offers education, resources, and funding to make a different choice. Governments in developed countries have no choice but to offer more options because the people have demanded it through proposing better solutions. When we ask for a change and offer ideas that can implement it, things get done. This has started to happen with our education, employment, and business development. People are able to follow ideas they love and create a life from it through offering it to others.

The only reason anyone stays in the rat race is because they choose not to explore these other options. What solutions will you offer through doing what you love?

Don't Chase The Rabbit

Words and thoughts often share a similar narration. We all have default thought patterns that, after the "high" of thinking positive for a few days, we may fall back to. That's ok; it's also part of the process. As we talked about in Emotional Self, it takes time for us to create new beliefs and patterns, and throughout that process, we have to go easy on ourselves.

Elliott Hulse is a strength coach, YouTube star, and overall fairly enlightened guy. I've been watching his videos for a long time and have seen his transition from being a fitness coach to a motivational speaker, wellness leader, and overall lifestyle hacker. This guy shares a lot of the principles in this book and has a really raw method of delivery. If you haven't watched anything by him yet, I suggest you look him up.

He has a very cool analogy he uses when it comes to entertaining thoughts that can also be used during meditation. Elliott says we can treat our thoughts like guests who come to our homes. When a guest comes that makes us feel good and treats us with respect, we might welcome them in, offer for them to stick around, and do our best to entertain them. On the other hand, when we have a guest that comes in and wreaks havoc on our home, makes us feel terrible, or creates chaos, we turn them away and say "not now."

We can also do this with our thoughts. Negative thoughts can bore their way in, no matter how hard we try to keep them out. This is where most people get overwhelmed and frustrated, eventually giving up. They think that the idea is to get to a place where the negative thoughts stop, and because they're so bombarded with them, they think they're a hopeless case and don't bother trying any longer. This is far from the truth. The potentially negative thoughts *never* stop in our lives, not ever. What changes is how we perceive and respond to them. Through continual practice, we get better at observing our negative thoughts and turning them away before we start to *think* them. The idea is to observe the thought and send it off before we allow ourselves to think it and follow it. I call this "chasing the rabbit". Take Elliott's advice and entertain the thoughts that serve you and turn the rest away. This concept can be used for our thoughts during meditation, as well.

Finding the Flow

The term flow I use comes from the idea of a "toroidal flow", which has its roots in a concept in geometry called the *torus*. The energy in a torus flows in through one end, circles around the center, and exits out the other side. Author Duane Elgin says that the torus is found in all patterns in nature from the atom to the universe itself.

The torus is a complicated concept to describe without an illustration, so I suggest, if interested, you do a quick internet search if you're able. Basically, the torus represents the recycling of energy and can be described by "what goes in must come out" and "what comes out must go in." It's a very fundamental concept in nature, metaphysics, and many other both spiritual and scientific concepts.

There are other terms that have explained this idea that you might be a little more familiar with. One of them is the concept of karma. Google defines karma as "the sum of a person's actions in this and previous states of existence, viewed as deciding their fate in future existences," or in other words "what goes out must come back". Basically, this means if you do crappy things, you'll experience crappy things, and if you do good things, you'll experience good things. The concept is a bit more complicated than this, but you get the idea.

There's another term that dates back thousands of years that's been used in a lot of Abrahamic religions such as Christianity and Judaism called "tithing". According to these religions, each person is expected to give a tithe, or tenth of their income, to the "church". The *church* may also be interpreted as the *community*. In many ancient texts, the word "church" comes from the Greek word Ekklesia, which does not have its roots in religion and directly translated means "assembly".

The practice of charity is rooted in every religion and spiritual belief that has ever existed. Furthermore, many of the most successful business people, religious or not, have admitted to practicing giving before receiving long before they've built their empires. Even Melchizedek asks for one tenth of Santiago's herd of sheep in order to find the hidden treasure in Paulo Coelho's *The Alchemist*. Giving before we receive is a very common concept used all over the world.

In his book, *"The strangest secret: how to live the life you desire"*, Earl Nightingale explains a theory called the Law of Prosperity. The idea is that if we are willing to work and provide to others, the universe will then reward us with prosperity, even if it doesn't come directly from those we worked for. Again, this concept is shared in many religious, spiritual, and success theories and beliefs throughout the world. By offering others our services, whatever they may be, will then be rewarded with prosperity. Sometimes it will come directly from the source in which we've offered our service, and sometimes it won't. Either way, it *will* come back to us.

A NOTE ON RELIGION

I've decided to keep references related to religion out of this book as much as possible. It's not because I have anything against religion. In fact, I believe there are very valuable philosophies in most religions. The position I hold is one of a complete open and inquisitive mind. My personal understanding and belief is that the majority of religions share the same general philosophy: love. Most religions have been rooted in the idea that the general intention for life is to love each other, ourselves, and our experiences. I've also come to believe that the majority of concepts related to this universal stuff also have some roots in some of the world's religions. Most of them share the idea of treating others well, having faith in yourself and your life, giving to others before you expect anything in return, working hard, and following your heart. So in saying all of this, I believe some or all of the concepts in this book can be integrated into any religion or no religion with the reader still having profound experiences. As always, take what you're willing and disregard what you need to.

What I'm pointing out here is that there seems to be a worldwide agreement that what you put out is what you're going to get back. Bob Proctor, Gregg Braden, Jack Canfield, Neale Donald Walsch, Jim Carrey, Will Smith, Oprah, Rhonda Byrne, and many others all share this idea. According to history, so have Henry Ford, Napoleon Hill, and many others. So, naturally, I had to put it to test.

There was a December not too long ago where I found myself in financial turmoil. I had about four hundred dollars left in the bank, one hundred dollars in change I'd saved up, and bills totalling around two thousand dollars coming out within a few days. I was stuck. I'd been reading a lot about giving and receiving and deeply researching the concepts of tithing and karma. From every religious and spiritual scripture I could find, as well as hundreds of other non-religious articles, the idea I gathered was simple. When you find yourself in need of something, you have to give it away. If you want love, give love. If you need money, give money. This all sounded great except how was I supposed to give money away when I didn't have what I needed in the first place? Regardless, all of the information I could find suggested that I *must* give in order to receive, despite how little I had. I had to have faith.

I thought, *what do I have to lose? If I keep what little I have, I still won't have enough for my bills, so it's worth a try. If I don't have it, I don't have it.* So that evening, I donated two hundred of the four hundred dollars I had left to an online charity, I bagged up all of the change around the house and took it downtown and gave it to every person I could find asking for money. It actually took me a little over an hour to give it all away. Each person I gave it to was completely overwhelmed with gratitude, and one woman even started crying. I still see her around, and she never lets me forget it.

The rest of this story is unbelievable, and I expect a lot of people to not accept it. I had a hard time accepting it myself. Within forty-eight hours, I had over two thousand dollars in the bank. I received an influx of clients without increasing any advertising (I had no money to anyway). I received a check in the mail for an unexpected government overcharge, and a drop in my insurance saving me two hundred dollars in bills. It was incredible.

The following month, I was getting close to being there again, so I immediately donated money to the first charity that resonated with me. The same thing happened. Since then, I've started donating at least 10 percent of my income *every month* and have experienced all different forms of abundance. I've also started giving away free products and coaching to complement the whole process and the abundance I receive on a weekly and even daily basis is nothing short of a continuous miracle.

For those who are financially stuck, this probably sounds like a terrifying idea; it was for me. Growing up, I knew what it meant to be poor, and the idea still scares me. But for some of the most successful people in the world, this is common practice and has been for hundreds of years. Charity has been a common bidding for all of history but seems to have lost its appeal with all of the fear that's pushed today. The difference is, *the rich don't wait to receive before they give.*

It sounds complicated, but it's really not. We don't stand in our gardens and say, "I'll plant a seed when the tomatoes start to grow", and we don't go to the fireplace and say, "give me heat, and I'll put some wood in", but for some reason, this is how we've been programmed to live our lives. I know it sounds crazy, but trust me, this is no joke.

Selfless Selfishness

I've had a lot of people ask me, "If you're giving just because you know you're going to get it back, isn't that selfish?" That's a fair point, but isn't that how you'd create the universe? Wouldn't you create it so that if people wanted something, they had to give something, as well? Otherwise, everyone would just go around taking things without giving anything back...hmm sounds familiar.

I call this selfless selfishness. It's a way for you to give because: 1) you know that because you're a contribution to the universe, the universe is going to take care of you and 2) because it feels great! There is no better feeling than giving someone something for **no** reason. It's euphoric. The feeling you get when you take someone by surprise with your love is second to none.

There's another side to the coin, though, which I've termed selfish selflessness. This is the type of act where you give something away to look good but still lead a selfish, self-centered life. You don't really care that someone feels good about it because you have what you want. This is an ugly side of giving that usually comes back in the form of pure unhappiness.

Take a Chance

I can't count how many times I've had someone motivated and ready to rock and roll only to completely lose them at this point. It's scary. I get it. I've been poor, jobless, and homeless. I'm not that person anymore, and I don't live by those restrictions.

Start small if you need to. Make a small donation at the grocery store or give something to the Salvation Army when you see them. Give change to the panhandler on the side of the road. It's not your business what they need it for, and your charity could be the significant event that changes their entire life. Ghandi said, "Be the change you want to see in the world".

I continually remind myself that the world I see outside is a product of what I believe inside, so I can't sit around and wait for someone else to fix the world's problems. The solutions come from each and every one of us. If every person in the world made one small act of selfless kindness each day, the world would be an incredibly different place. I *promise* you, if you incorporate these ideas into your life, no matter how small, you will see change. I make that promise because I don't believe it, I know it. Try it out, do what you can.

Come-unity

The concept of giving doesn't just pertain to money. As I mentioned in my story earlier, abundance can come in all forms. Some of us may find ourselves in a position where it seems that giving any money is nearly impossible; that's ok. Giving can also mean giving love, giving time (AKA volunteering), giving belongings, or even giving advice and inspiration. Put yourself in the mind space of giving, no matter what the object you're giving is, and work your way up as you can.

Once we've started practicing giving, we also need to practice the other side of the coin. Some of us may experience a bit of resistance here and will find ourselves faced with the challenge of letting go of pride. The practice I'm referring to is that of *receiving*. With my upbringing, despite the amount of times I've used food banks or soup kitchens, I've still had a hard time asking for something when I need it and not feeling immense guilt after I got it. Anytime someone would do something for me, I'd feel this burning guilt to say, "I'll pay you back", or "next time it's on me". While I really encourage doing nice things for anyone you can, I strongly discourage attaching guilt to any of the times where you experience abundance. There's only one thing you need to say when someone gives you something, whether it's a compliment or a car: Thank You. Remind yourself that you are practicing the flow of giving and receiving, and that the person who is giving you something will also receive abundance in all forms because of *their* practice. This doesn't mean you can't be grateful or appreciative; it simply means make sure your reactions are out of love and not guilt.

There was a time I was going to buy a Himalayan Salt lamp for my home, and I had a playful idea. I decided I'd post a status on Facebook that said, "Where can I buy a Himalayan Salt lamp?" After about three comments, someone posted and said, "I have one that you can have!" This is abundance. I gratefully accepted the offer.

This concept of giving and receiving is really about community. It's about creating relationships with people and doing your part. In my first twenty-four months in nutrition coaching, I spent very little in advertising. My clients came from friends of friends and colleagues. Any chance I got, I would give away free plans for donations, offer discounts to those who were financially stuck, or put on free seminars.

We're moving away from a time of separation and moving in to a time of unity. Doing for others is not only a great way to ensure you have everything you need, but it is an incredible way of distracting you from whatever it is you could be stressed or worried about. It's nearly impossible to feel crappy when you're doing something for someone else. Don't believe me? Try it. Next time you're feeling broke, overwhelmed, or in over your head, try doing something for someone else.

The level of abundance you experience in your life will be directly related to the size of your social network. The more people you know and help the more people that will help you. That doesn't mean you need to get out and meet every person you can just to see what you can get out of them, and it also doesn't mean that you have to overwhelm yourself trying to maintain hundreds of close relationships. It simply means that becoming a sociable person and being genuine and authentic to those you do meet will ensure a healthy social life and increase your experience of abundance. Sometimes friendships fade, and our close relationships slowly drift apart, but that doesn't make them any less real. I have many friends who I may not see for a year or more, but when we meet, it's like we never parted. Don't limit your relationships with people, be genuine and considerate, and you'll experience a level of abundance you never knew possible.

Be the Vibes

Our reality really is a reflection of our internal state, so it's important for us to imagine ways we can *be* the vibrations we want to experience. Ways of practicing this might be taking the role of inspiration for others and helping their dreams come true. How can you inspire someone else? What things can you say or do that will help them make their dream a reality? I experience this all of the time and have had incredible mentors that have connected me with just the right person to make something happen, so in turn, I try my best to be this inspiration for others any chance I get.

When we live in the vibration of what it is we want to experience, we can't help but manifest it. It works when we're living in the vibration of stress and fear, but it also works when we're living in the vibration of love, abundance, and gratitude. When someone asks you for change, and you give it to them, you are *their* form of abundance. In turn, you will manifest your own form of abundance. When you give someone your love, you are vibrating as love. The same principle applies to having gratitude. When you receive someone in your life, no matter how small, say *thank you.* This is also a practice that has been around for thousands of years. How hard is it to say thank you? Thank you, thank you, thank you! Seems easy to me.

Affirmative

Affirmations can be a great tool in sending out the right vibrations for our manifestation. Essentially, an affirmation is a sentence or statement that describes the type of state you're looking to manifest. A simple example might be, "I manifest wealth and abundance easily". In my experience, the most effective affirmations are those that are written or spoken in words that you actually use. If you're using words that never appear in your vocabulary, it's going to be hard for you to believe it. Keep it simple, and say what you really mean. Be sure to make your affirmations definitive statements rather than polite suggestions, and integrate the level of effort it will take.

"I *easily and effortlessly* manifest abundance in my life."

"I *am* the creator of my reality and my dreams manifest *with ease.*"

"I *will* live in alignment with my higher self and manifest my desires *effortlessly.*"

Note: In the next element, Creative Visualization, I mention that you should create goals that are big and may take a bit longer to manifest, as well as short term goals that will manifest quickly. Affirmations are best for these short-term goals. If you keep telling yourself that you're going to manifest your dream car but haven't gotten your license yet, chances are you're going to lose your steam and stop believing it. Dream the big dream, but take the necessary steps to get there.

It Comes From The Heart

In The Shift, we discuss the concept that our hearts produce an electromagnetic force five thousand times stronger than our minds. Though our thoughts are powerful and can travel globally, our *feelings* are significantly more powerful and make a much bigger impact on the reality we experience. When we're saying affirmations or utilizing the other manifestation practices we'll discuss in the next element, we need to really feel it. This also applies to practicing giving and receiving. We are emotional animals, more than just monkeys with awareness. Though we don't want to stew on emotions, allow yourself to freely feel them, bad and good, because this is what makes us human and ultimately what makes us creators. Pat yourself on the back, cry at movies, smile like a goofball. There's no shame in showing who we really are at the core.

A Final Note On Lack

As we mentioned in Emotional Self, fear is a primitive emotion, and it's important to realize that fear of not having enough, be it money, love, or anything, is an illusion that we're *choosing* to no longer observe. We have broken through the illusory construct and see it for what it is. Through understanding this, we can realize that fear is a prison with holographic bars that can only hold you so long as you let them. We know that we must challenge our fears and question their reality. We must experience the truth and dispel the illusion. Choose to no longer be a victim, and realize that your higher potential already exists and is waiting for you to align with it.

My Practice

Becoming mindful of the vibration we're exchanging is one of the most important aspects of actualizing our dreams. I make it a point to be very mindful of the words I'm using and the conversations I'm having. I try my best to never participate in drama or fear-based conversations, and when I do, I try my best to quickly think of solutions I'd like to manifest. I watch very, very little TV and don't watch or read the mainstream news, but when I *do* hear of something going on in the world that I don't like, I find ways I can contribute, no matter how small.

There are endless methods to donate your time or small amounts of money to any type of cause that resonates with you. When I feel a bit lonely or pessimistic, I might volunteer at a soup kitchen or give some change to some panhandlers. Many of us dream of a world where we all get along, but the first step happens with each of us alone. We have the ability inside to create a beautiful world around us, and it starts with our vibratory exchange. What vibrations are you putting out?

Homework

Curious Creator – any 3   Master Manifestor – all

1) **Donate.** Give money, anywhere. I like to give to those who need it most, so follow your intuition. It could be the panhandler you walk by every day, the charity volunteer bagging your groceries, or some other person or group who resonates with you.

2) **Donate monthly.** If you really want to see what level of abundance you can manifest in your life, then take a chance and donate monthly. Choose one organization or many, one person or a group. Whatever you do, do it monthly. You can find lots of great charities at www.canadahelps.org

3) **Volunteer.** Your time is valuable, so give some of it away. Every little bit makes a huge difference.

4) **Create a dream team.** Lend some friends your copy of this book, or buy it for them, then create a dream team. Practice the skill of positive redirection on each other. Remember, there is power in numbers.

5) **Write a daily gratitude list.** Being grateful for what you have will bring you more of it. Write ten things you're grateful for at the beginning or end of everyday (or both!). We will be creating a daily gratitude app soon through www.whataretheelements.com so stay posted!

Visualize this thing that you want, see it, feel it, believe in it.
Make your mental blue print, and begin to build.

-Robert Collier

Element 4

<u>Creative Visualization</u>

When I meet someone new, one of my favorite questions to ask them is, "If money didn't matter, how would you contribute to the world? Which of your talents could the world use more of?" Most people blush or smirk before answering, if they answer at all. Whatever the answer, though, this is almost always their true calling. This is their life's purpose.

Deep down, we all have this innate, burning idea within us that is boring its way into our hearts, catching our attention at every turn. There is that one thing, or maybe those many things, you knew you were born to do, if only you had the time off work or the money to get started. The thing is we don't need to wait for the time off work or the money to begin our journey. The creation begins the moment we have an idea.

"I always tell people that revelling in big ideas, for me, is kind of like an antidote to existential angst."

-Jason Silva

Filmmaker and futurist, Jason Silva, has a lot of ideas he likes to talk about with one of my favorites being the idea of ideas. Jason talks about how ideas are like fire. Fire can destroy homes and leave ash where there was once love. However, if you can domesticate and refine fire, you can send a man to the moon. Ideas, in many ways, are like fire.

But where does an idea come from? Is it a thing, like a pebble or a blade of grass? Or are ideas simply a carrot on a stick that can distract us until our inevitable demise? I like to believe that ideas are the directional manifestation of our higher purpose. Or in other words, ideas are the inspiration from within—the voice that whispers in our ears, "It's this way".

Every incredible invention, culturally changing movement, or beautiful piece of music was once simply an idea. It was a minute speck in the infinitely vast ocean of concepts. Ideas then might be thought of as one of the first condensed expressions of pure potential.

The tricky question isn't so much what an idea is, but rather where it came from. I think humans like to carry the idea that "I" thought the idea, but did you really? Did you consciously choose to think of the idea, or did it come to you almost out of nowhere, in which time you elaborated on it and began to conceptualize its details? This question sort of brings us back to the idea of consciousness. If consciousness is the infinite ocean of all possibility and probability, then all of our ideas would have to be within that ocean, and therefore, they must have come from somewhere else, somewhere within. Then once the idea has "sparked" within our conscious mind, we take it and run with it, molding and forming it into the intricately detailed concepts we create.

The reason I want to explore the idea of ideas is so that we can start to understand exactly how important they are in regards to our creation. Without them, we would simply be living day by day in search of food, water, shelter, and reproduction with nothing more to our lives. Ideas are part of the essence of what it is that makes us human. Entire countries have been formed on the foundation of an idea. Steve Jobs and Apple revolutionized the way we communicate with an idea. The words you're reading right now are the product of an inspired idea. Ideas elevate the human experience into high definition.

Dancing with the Darkness

The first step in actually deciding what it is we're looking to create in our lives is acknowledging and responding to our ideas. Our ideas can come seemingly out of nowhere; they can even come in response to a situation that creates discomfort. They'll spawn out of the contrast in our experience. Unfortunately, most of the time, we perceive our contrasting experiences as misfortune or "negative".

We see examples of this every day, but a clear one might be an unhappy relationship. When we're subjectively experiencing the relationship, we might feel that we're incredibly unlucky and wonder why we're the ones who have to suffer in having it. Maybe the person we're with seemed like the perfect fit at one time, but after time, we realize there's no connection, and they don't share the passions we have for things in our lives now. Within this relationship, we feel like we're wasting time, missing out on true love. What we seldom realize is that this relationship is serving as a pivot point, helping us learn what it is we *do* want through experiencing that which we don't.

Through experiencing the relationship we don't want, we become more accurate conceivers and creators of the relationship we *do* want. Some relationships are meant to be for long periods of time, and some are meant to bring us lessons. These lessons help us become better people and more accurate creators because we know what works for us. If we've never tried ice cream, we can't possibly know that we prefer chocolate over vanilla, but through trying them both and not liking one, can we refine that preference.

Contrast in our lives happens all of the time and continually creates opportunities to spark an idea. Maybe we got let go at a job or got an overdue bill notice in the mail. For a moment, we pause and think of what it would be like "if just..." It's in these moments we become creators and start to imagine a better world for us and those around us, full of excitement and happiness. Unfortunately, our old patterns and beliefs often come up, putting us back into our mammalian brain—back into fear.

I can't possibly count how many ideas I have in the run of a day, and many of them are generated from an experience of contrast. They could be completely far-fetched (if there is such a thing), and some seem a bit more within reach. Either way, without actually acting on these ideas, nothing would ever happen. In his book, *"The 4 Hour Work Week"*, Tim Ferris says, "'Someday' is a disease that will take your dreams to the grave with you." This concept also applies perfectly to inspired ideas. If something comes to you, and you think there's even an inkling of a chance that it could become something, then you *need* to act on it.

The Rule of 72... Seconds

The Rule of 72 is a rule in economics that helps determine how long an investment will take to double your money. When it comes to ideas I use "the rule of 72 seconds." Within seventy-two seconds of an idea, there should be something done about it; write it down in a journal, brainstorm names or even tell it to a friend. Put a little bit of life and imagination into the idea, no matter how crazy it sounds. Spend at least seventy-two seconds imagining this idea being real and exploring all of the potentials. Through putting this intention out there, you're planting a seed in the universe, creating a strong, vibratory intention.

After you've become good at the rule of seventy-two seconds, start actually writing down goals for your ideas, even if they're small. Although it's heavily suggested to dream the biggest dream possible, it's also important to set incremental milestones. If the most you've ever made for a yearly salary is forty thousand dollars, it may be hard to visualize yourself being a millionaire in five years. It does not mean it's not possible; it just means you're unexposed to that level of lifestyle so far. Create incremental lists of goals that flow toward your greatest excitement. What would life as a millionaire be like? What would you be, have, and do? Is it the actual money you desire or what you think the money can bring you? Maybe it's the perceived lifestyle of a millionaire that you really want. If so, start imagining the aspects of the lifestyle you'd like for yourself.

I will.

One of my favorite Creative Visualization practices is an "I will" list. This is a list of goals and lifestyle changes I plan for my life. An item on the list might be, "I will finish writing my book by December 2014", or "I will own a home in California by April 2016". I will create incremental, short-term goals and large, long-term goals. I will continually change my list, adding new items and erasing achieved or changed items. Some items will expire, and some will be completed before the expected date. My personal success rate is between 70-80 percent completion when on the list, and these aren't always simple tasks.

SIDENOTE: There are some beliefs that creating intentions and desires on the New Moon can increase the likelihood of their manifestation. This has been used for thousands of years by farmers when planting seeds for a new crop. I don't personally follow strictness with things like this, but if it interests you, maybe consider looking into it!

I choose the words "I will" instead of "I want" because "want" is future tense. Want is something that implies you may not get it. *Want* is for those who are asking permission, and *will* is for those who don't need it. When you desire from the heart, the universe responds best to decisive proclamations, not polite requests. Though your subconscious mind may try to bring up old, ego-based patterns and beliefs, telling you that it's a foolish desire or unrealistic, you must push through and continue with the effort. Eventually, your mind will reprogram, and you will begin to release the parking brake.

In 1984, Russia started implementing creative visualization techniques into their Olympic athletes' training camps, and it worked incredibly. The study concluded that those who spent 25 percent of their time doing physical training and 75 percent of the time doing visualization training had more success than those doing 100 percent physical training. When athletes were hooked up to brain imaging software, many researchers concluded that the same area of the brain would become active during visualization as during physical activity. This basically means that we can create familiar neural pathways in our brains without actually partaking in the physical activity itself.

This practice works because the subconscious mind gets fed information from our imagination and processes it. It doesn't know whether it's real or not; it simply processes it as it comes. That means whether you're imagining how to hit a home run or deliver a perfect presentation, your subconscious mind will believe it to be true.

The subconscious mind doesn't just receive information, though; it also sends it out. As we program our subconscious mind to believe the ideas we're feeding it, it will in turn send them out into the universe to be manifested. This is why it's so important to be mindful of the stories we tell ourselves.

In 1937, Napoleon Hill wrote the book, *"Think and Grow Rich"*. At the time of his death in 1970, this book had already sold twenty million copies, and by 2011, over seventy million copies had been sold. It has inspired countless manifestation books after it, including *"The Law of Attraction"* by Esther and Jerry Hicks, as well as *"The Secret"* by Rhonda Byrne. In this book, he continually repeats the phrase, "What the mind of man can conceive and believe, it can achieve". He even mentions how our internal vibrations are sent out into the ether to be manifested. Again, this book was written in 1937! If you haven't read it yet, I would strongly suggest you do.

A great practice to reinforce your desires is using various dream cues. Dream cues can be pictures, post-it notes, smart phone and computer wallpapers, or any type of item that you will see throughout your day that will remind you of your desire. One popular example is a vision board. A vision board is a bulletin board, white board, or any other type of board you put somewhere in your home that you're going to see often. On this board, you can put various objects that represent your desire. Maybe it's a check to you from yourself dated for next year, a picture of your dream car, or even a Photoshopped version of your dream bank account balance. Use your imagination!

Long before anyone knew who he was comedian Jim Carrey used to drive to Hollywood and stare at the houses, imagining which one would be his. He would picture himself living in them. Jack Canfield would tack a check for one million dollars on the ceiling above his bed so it was the first thing he saw when he woke up. Countless of the world's most successful people all claim to have spent lots of time imagining their dreams long before they ever happened. They created it in their mind then watched it manifest in their lives.

Know Your Desire

It's important to understand what it is we really desire. We might *think* something is what we desire but in fact it's just a *symbol* of our desire. An example might be a really nice car. The question should be is it really the car that you want, or is it the lifestyle that the car represents? If so, what type of lifestyle is that? Is it financial independence? Is it feeling passionate and happy every day? Is it comfortably providing for your family? It's very important to understand the lifestyle associated with our material and emotional desires so that we are more focused on the actual desired state, rather than the material items that represent it. Oftentimes, our surface desires are just the tip of the iceberg for something deeper, and when we learn what that is, we might realize we're closer than we imagined. Always ask yourself, is this a surface desire or a true desire? For example, if you were able to manifest the dream car, could you keep up with its maintenance and repairs? If not, then perhaps a deeper desire is one of financial independence where you can eventually easily afford things like nice cars and other toys. With financial independence, we could also help our families as well as the less fortunate.

When we know what our true desires are, we pair the mind with our hearts. When we desire something that is true to us, we spark a passionate flame inside that gives us fuel far beyond the mind alone. Our words and thoughts are simply expressions of our feelings. Our hearts are the true navigational systems for our dream life.

Homework Break

I want you to take moment right now and write down exactly who you want to be in a year from now. Write down where you'll live, who you'll spend your time with, and what types of activities you'll engage in. Don't be humble here, be very *unrealistic*. Make sure you're clear and spare no details. Live in this dream for a moment. If you can't do this right now, make sure you do it as soon as possible. Do not skip this. Being accountable is one of the most important traits of the successful.

Are We Creating New Realities?

Each time we imagine something, we create a new possible outcome. We create a universe with the potential you've imagined. When you dream about the house, the car, and the vacations, you're making them all possible. They're now existing simultaneously with the universe you're in right now, and quantum shifting is how you're going to get there. (Not familiar with quantum shifting? We discuss it in The Shift).

Through continually visualizing your dream life, editing, changing, and molding it, you're moving in alignment with that potential "you". You're *shifting* into that reality. This is where the idea of the law of attraction and quantum shifting somewhat differ. I've created an image below to show how a shift like this may occur. Reality A is the current reality, where you're struggling to pay for bills, making dinner for one, continually feeling stuck at your job, or getting close to feeling like you're succeeding but being too afraid to pull the trigger. In reality B, you're living the dream. Your bills are all caught up, and if for some reason they get behind, you know everything will work out. Your friendships and relationships are healthy, and you feel surrounded by people you truly care about and who care about you. You get things you want and need almost with ease and without money, though money always seems to be there. You're doing what you love and know that if money was no object, you'd be doing the same thing.

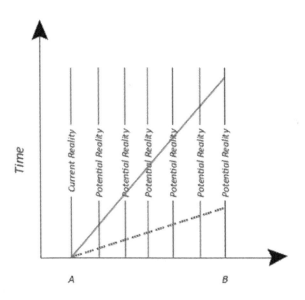

If you're currently in reality A and you want to shift to reality B, you'll have to really imagine what reality B is going to look like, what it *will be* like. You have to creatively visualize what "you" in reality B are going to wear, how you're going to treat others, what state your home will be in and how you will react to emotional and personal struggles. You have to try to *feel* what you'll feel like in that reality. The solid line represents one path you may take to reality B, and the dotted line represents another. The difference between these two relies on the foundation you build with your emotional and physical self, your exchange of frequency and vibration, as well as your ability to creatively intend that reality to exist. The time delay between realities A and B will be heavily dependent on your Personal Alignment and blockages, all of which, we discuss in the later Elements.

This idea of connecting with a different you isn't a new concept. There are a lot of books and programs already out there that offer suggestions to do just that, including Burt Goldman's concept called "Quantum Jumping", which has been used on over forty thousand students worldwide. Burt claims that, through using meditative visualization, you can visit a version of yourself in your imagination and learn the skills they have that you want. Perhaps they're a great musician, business person, or artist. According to Quantum Jumping, you can meet this version of yourself and absorb their skills.

Are you actually visiting versions of yourself during Quantum Jumping? That's hard to say, but in the least, you're partaking in a very deep, intricate version of creative visualization.

Visualization Transcendence

Though Quantum Jumping may be an effective method of visualization, you don't necessarily need to subscribe to that method to get the desired outcome. Meditating for a few minutes before beginning your visualization practice can offer incredible results. Russia started this practice over thirty years ago for their Olympic athletes, but martial artists have been doing this for thousands of years. Simply start off by using standard focus techniques such as focusing on your breathing or even binaural beats for five to ten minutes. Once in a deep state of meditation, you can start visualizing your desire vividly. Continue for as long as you like, truly living in that moment, experiencing everything you might experience if it were actually happening. Repeat this a couple of times a week, or even daily if you desire.

Dreamer, You Know You Are a Dreamer

As children, we have incredible, unlimited imaginations, but as we get older we're told to "grow up" and "be realistic". It's this type of thinking that limits our ability to create magnificent, magical worlds for ourselves and those around us. We could blame our parents, the education system, the post-secondary schools, or the workforce, but they didn't know what we know. They didn't have the resources we're learning now. Luckily, our imagination is still there, buried deep inside, waiting for a nice jump-start. With a little bit of push, we can fire it up and have it running smoothly in no time.

I'm inviting you to try to put yourself back in that place of unlimited potential for a little bit of everyday. Be unrealistic and put your head in the clouds. Dream of a world full of goose bumps, goofy smiles, and happy tears. Imagine a world where your troubles are just obstacles making you quicker on your feet and leading to bigger and better things. Create something unforgettable in your mind and watch it manifest in front of your eyes.

My Practice

I have a few visualization practices that I've turned into regular habit. I update my "I Will" list almost on a weekly basis, and I continually write down my dreams on a free journal application on my phone. Whenever I think of an idea, I try to think of two or three points about it and write them down. I have a white board above my kitchen table where I put anything that I need a daily reminder for, and I never ignore an inspired thought. This book was once a basic idea that has changed names and structure many times, but anytime I thought about it, I wrote down any of the details I could. I look up vacation spots, imagine details about businesses I want to start, and daydream all of the time. The only limitation to our dreams is the range of our imagination. How big will you dream?

Homework

Curious Creator – any 3   Master Manifestor – all

1) **Dream.** Write a paragraph or two describing what type of dream life you're going to have. Be detailed and live in that for a moment.

2) **I will.** Write a list of things you will achieve and when you will achieve them by. Write it like, "I will _____ by _____". Update this list often (bi-weekly for me, most of the time).

3) **Consult the board.** Create a dream board (or vision board) somewhere in your home. This can be a bulletin board or a magnetic white board (my favorite) where you write and post reminders about your dreams.

4) **Visualize.** Spend some time every day visualizing your dream, even if it's only for a moment. If you really want to take it to the next level, then start by meditating for five to ten minutes first. You can find lots of free guided meditation videos and MP3s on my website at www.rickygoodall.com

5) **Dance with darkness.** Name three situations in your life that seemed terrible but ended up leading to a greater state of happiness and/or excitement. How has your life changed because of them?

"Life wants you to live in total alignment with true love, passion and integrity."

-Bryant McGill

ELEMENT 5

PERSONAL ALIGNMENT

Imagine for a moment that you're sailing across the world. You've set sail in Nova Scotia, Canada, and you're planning to sail to Europe. You pack your bags, secure the life boats, top off the reserve fuel, and notify your loved ones of your adventure. You lift the anchor and begin your journey.

You've been sailing for weeks and have spent lots of time reading, meditating, and imagining all of the amazing things you're going to do when you get to Europe. As the dawn breaks one day, you look ahead and see land. You're not only amazed that you've made it but shocked that you've gotten there in such incredible time. You're far ahead of schedule and will have time to do much more than expected.

As you get closer to land, you see houses and a town. You dock your boat, excited to get off the ocean for a moment. You walk up to the first people you see and overhear them speaking in a familiar language. In fact, it sounds like perfect English. You're ecstatic! You approach them with an eagerness to socialize and share your excitement. As you're about to greet the first group, you see a car and glance at the license plate. The plate displays, "MAINE 3847 PF Vacationland."

"Wait, this must be a mistake," you proclaim. You look at another vehicle, "MAINE 4657 TH", and another, "MAINE 4239 FG". You stop the first person you see and ask, "Where are we?" The puzzled gentleman replies, "Earth, pal, where do you think?"

As your heart sinks and your face flushes with embarrassment, you realize you've been sailing in circles on the ocean, making it only a few hundred kilometers from home. As you head back to your boat, you realize that the issue is clear; your navigational equipment is out of whack, and you never had a chance. Your alignment was completely off.

Alignment on the ocean is just as important as alignment in our lives. If we're not properly aligned with the life we desire, then we're going to find ourselves going in circles, often ending up either somewhere completely unintended or worse—right back where we started. Taking conscious action toward our desires and living in alignment with our dreams will ensure we are heading in the right direction.

Building a strong emotional and physical self, vibrating in harmony with our environment, and creatively visualizing our desires are all very important and are essentially the foundation for the rest of what's to come. Even the most fuel efficient and reliable vehicle needs proper direction.

In order to live in alignment with our dreams, we have to be prepared to be honest with how much we are willing to commit to them. We have to be willing to step out of our comfort zone and do something different. One of my favorite quotes by Henry

Ford is, "If you always do what you've always done, you'll always get what you've always got". If we continue to live in alignment with the life we *don't* want, then we will never manifest the life we *do* want. This can be where it gets tricky for some people.

To adjust into alignment with the life of our dreams, we have to start to imagine what our lives will be like when we get there. How will this future version of you conduct yourself? How will you react to situations? How will you dress, speak, eat, and exercise? These are all very important questions you must ask yourself. In our first element, Emotional Self, we started to question our fears and beliefs and challenge their existence. We began to no longer accept patterns and habits that didn't serve us, and we began to create new ones that do. This is the beginning of our transformation; this is when we start to live in alignment with our desires.

When we question our fears and beliefs, we can start to change how we react to situations. It's easy to be mindful of our thoughts, words, and actions when everything is going well, but it's not always so easy when disaster hits. When our emotions start to take over and our intelligent mind decides to take a nap, it's easy to revert back to old habits. It is here where we can really start to challenge our growth, however.

Through becoming more conscious of our old habits when they arise and realizing that they are simply aspects of our old self trying to survive, we can consciously shift back into alignment with the new version of ourselves. We can begin to change habits, forge new patterns, and rewire the brain. This takes determination, consistency, and patience. It also requires humility and forgiveness. When we've allowed an old habit to surface, our immediate reaction is to beat ourselves up and get stuck in the self-destructive cycle of, "Oh here I go again, screwing everything up. How typical." It's this negative self-talk that only reinforces the old patterns.

The new, evolved version of you knows that these patterns are a manifestation of the *old* self and will simply observe them as an area for growth. The new you will see them as just another challenge to overcome and will feel gratitude for it coming to the surface now rather than later. The new you loves challenges because every challenge presents new and exciting opportunities for growth and an elevated sense of self.

As we grow and begin to change old habits, we might deceive ourselves into thinking that old habit is completely gone forever. We think it has somehow disappeared, never to be seen again. Then when something happens, and we slip up, we beat ourselves up, feeling the ultimate pain of defeat. The problem exists only in the understanding of the habit in the first place.

When we change a pattern or a habit, we are not erasing it forever, but we are allowing it to heal, much like a deep cut or an incision. If looked at closely enough, the scar may still be visible. This doesn't mean that we are still injured or that our insides are going to fall out at any given moment. It simply means that the area was once jeopardized and needs to be treated with care. Over time, the scar fades, and the body becomes stronger. Our minds work the same way.

Through continually adjusting our alignment with our dreams, we are reinforcing new habits and beliefs, making it easier for our future selves to stay in alignment. If you've cut down from one cheeseburger a day to one every couple of days, then in a few weeks, it will be easy for you to go from one every couple of days to one a week. As you incrementally shift your alignment closer and closer to your desired manifestation, you will experience a much better representation of the new you. This change may take time, or it may come quickly. The important thing is to be honest with yourself while continuing to push to the edge of your comfort zone.

Who Are You?

Our next question is clear. Who are you, and who do you want to be? Do you want to be a famous rock star? Do you want to be the CEO of a Fortune 500 company? Do you want to backpack the world? We've covered these questions in Creative Visualization, and I like to think of this chapter as the bridge from imagination to manifestation. This chapter is how you're going to make your dream a reality.

Once you've established who you want to be and what you want to be doing in your future, it's time to get a little bit more detailed. It's time to start incrementally shifting toward your future self. One example is a race car driver. If your dream is to be a race car driver, but you've never even driven a car, then I think it's obvious what your first incremental shift is. Start by getting creative and honest about the steps you need to take to shift into alignment with your manifestation.

The most important first step is to actually believe it's possible. Some of the most successful people in the world *knew* they were going to become successful before they ever did. One of the best examples I always use is Muhammad Ali and his famous quote, "I'm the greatest. I said that even before I knew I was". These types of people *lived* the part long before they ever became it.

There's a technique in marketing called "the boy band principle", which is also used in many relationship and attraction coaching practices. The idea is that most boy bands have photo shoots taken and videos filmed with tonnes of screaming fans chasing them, showering them with love and acting star struck long before the boy band ever becomes famous or anyone knows who they are. The idea is that they're creating the *belief* that they're famous, and therefore, others believe it. They're "faking it until they make it". Our subconscious mind works the same way.

If you continually reinforce the idea that you are the rock star, the Fortune 500 CEO, or the race car driver, then you will start to act in accordance and in alignment with these types of people. In sales, we're told to "dress for success". By dressing in a professional manner, we *feel* successful before we even step out the door. We start to believe that we *are* successful then make decisions and actions that align accordingly. On the other hand, if you desire to be these things but continually neglect your hygiene, sleep in until one o'clock p.m., or play video games for hours every day, then chances are your dreams aren't going to manifest too quickly—if at all. Unless, of course, your dream is to be a late night video game tester. Then maybe you are living the dream.

You already know what you want to be or do, and if you're reading this book, I hope you're starting to believe it's possible. The next step is starting to align your life with that dream. It's time to start living that lifestyle, even if only a little bit at a time. Like any transition, there are going to be challenges, and you're going to have to get out of your comfort zone, but it can definitely be done. When I was nineteen years old, I used to go to the call center I worked at dressed in a hand knit sweater with brown corduroy pants and a hands-free corded headset I got for one dollar. I had a hair style I paid less than ten dollars for months before and twenty-year-old dress shoes I had gotten at a thrift store. I was not dressed for success. Imagine a clear image of who you want to be and strive to be that person. Rather than fake it until you make it, *believe* it until you *become* it.

Paint a Picture

If you have a dream in mind, then you have an idea who that future self will be, and if you did your homework earlier, you have also written it down. To expand on this assignment, make a list of attributes this future version of you will have. Will they dress well? Will they get plenty of rest? Will they spend time with loved ones? Will they enjoy their work, whether for themselves or someone else? Will they be healthy? Make a list and spare no details. Paint a clear, vivid picture of who this person is going to be. In Creative Visualization, I got you to imagine your dream in detail. Now I'm asking you to imagine the dreamer in detail. Who will you be?

Once you've written out a detailed list of whom you're going to be in your dream, then it's time to take a current inventory of where you are now. Uh oh. I know that might be a bit intimidating, but don't worry. The first step to changing something is knowing what to change. That's what we're here for—that's why you're reading this book.

Once you've finished the list of the attributes, you're going to have to then write a list of the current attributes you're going to change to get there. If the future you dresses well, then maybe the current you will be more patient trying on clothes or will throw out the jeans with the ripped crotch (seriously, throw them out). If the future you is going to be a business owner, then maybe the current you is going to stop being irresponsible with money and is going to spend less time in front of the TV or browsing social media.

It's important to be honest about where you are in order to get to where you want to be. This isn't an exercise in shame—it's an exercise in honesty and accountability. If you feel guilt coming up for how far you are from your dream, let it go. It doesn't serve you or help you get to where you're going. Remember, it's a manifestation of your previous thoughts, choices, and actions.

Once you've established where you want to be and where you

are, then we can start to fill in the middle a little bit. Now we can start to work on the incremental changes. If not careful, however, this is where some people get a little overzealous and set themselves up for failure. If your dream is to be a Kickboxing Champion but you've never Kickboxed, though it's a good idea to start taking lessons, it's *not* a good idea to jump into a routine fit for an experienced champion. Set realistic, incremental markers that may be a little bit ambitious but are still within a healthy reach.

One useful practice is to write out a time-based goal list that's broken into time blocks. Maybe you'll write out where you want to be next week, next month, in three months, in six months, in one year, and so on. I don't personally write anything longer than a year or two, because frankly, I change way too much, and in many ways, it can limit my dream potential. My "I Will" list usually extends into the following year or so. If you'd like, you can split your "I Will" list into these time-based blocks and even organize it as things you will do, be, or have.

Lifestyle Budgets

This practice has proven to become one of my most useful to date. Setting a lifestyle budget is a perfect way to be sure you're living in alignment with your dream. This works both in terms of a *minimum* budget and a *maximum* budget. One very important aspect of dream manifestation that many people miss is setting a minimum level of lifestyle you're willing to live in order to push you to the next level. If your dream is to become a millionaire, but you penny pinch over gas going up a couple of cents, then you're not really living in the place of ease, happiness, and financial independence that a millionaire would.

On the other hand, if you're buying multiple lattes every day, wasting money on material items you don't need, and eating out too often, then this is also not how most millionaires live, especially as they're building their empires. Remember that we want to *incrementally* shift to our desires. If your dream is to be a millionaire, but right now you make thirty thousand dollars per year, then let's set a budget that allows you to feel freedom while also keeping your end goal in mind. Successful people usually spend wisely.

By the way, I don't use actual dollar amounts when setting my lifestyle budget. For example, each week, I have a Victory Meal, and the last thing I want to worry about is whether I pay ten dollars or fifty dollars for it. It's my Victory Meal, and I earned it, so whatever meal I desire that week, I'm going to eat. It may sound contradictory to the paragraph above, but it's also important to not feel guilty for your rewards. If you decide that this week you're going to a five star restaurant and spending fifty dollars on a meal, then accept that and enjoy it.

The guilt is from the fear of lack and what we fear we must manifest into our experience. Perhaps, for the first couple of months, you have decided you experience too much guilt when you spend big, so you're going to limit your spending to something just above what you're used to; that's ok, too. Just make sure that your lifestyle budget is still pushing the edge of your comfort zone so you can increase that style of living.

Some examples for lifestyle budget items might be your Victory Meals, the amount of coffees you buy each day, entertainment activities with the family, vacations, clothing, or new household items. Whatever it may be, set a budget for it and stick to it. This means that not only do you not go over the budget; you also don't go *under* it. If money seems tight this week, then you should *still* go for that movie with your spouse. This will help reinforce the belief and the *knowingness* that you are a creator, and though money may seem tight, abundance is plentiful, and you are no longer a prisoner of that fear. Through having faith in the process, you bring it to your reality.

Another example could be your donations and volunteer activities. Remember, budget doesn't mean limitation, it means a standard of living. Your lifestyle budget should be the minimum and maximum for any activities that are conducive to your future. They can include exercise classes, music lessons, daily writing, and personal commitments. Anything and everything that is going to help you shift into alignment with your manifestation should be on your lifestyle budget.

Dream Routines

Dream Routines take the lifestyle budget just a step further. A Dream Routine can be a daily, weekly, or monthly routine that helps you stay accountable to your lifestyle budget. I don't create yearly dream routines because the items are usually too far apart to be accountable for. When I started using Dream Routines, I created a to-do checklist with an application on my phone. I could check it and uncheck it without completely deleting the item, so it would stay on the list. I created a Daily Dream Routine list, a Weekly Dream Routine list, and a Monthly Dream Routine list. My Daily Dream Routine included things like meditate, have one coffee out, read for thirty minutes, do one nice thing, write a gratitude list, write one thousand words on the book, exercise, use a foam roller, etc.

My Weekly Dream Routine listed items like have one Victory Meal, try a new recipe, donate, try a new exercise class, or visit the local market. There's really no limit to what you can use these lists for, and having something that keeps you accountable every day is an easy way to stay in alignment with your dreams.

Dream Routines can also be used to break habits or create new ones. An example might be someone who is trying to quit smoking. The Daily Dream Routine could have a check item that says, "Have One Cigarette", or it could even have one that says, "Be Healthy All Day". By having this option there to check off, you are giving yourself an emotional reward at the end of every day. You'll note that rather than write, "Have No Cigarettes", I suggest "Be Healthy All Day". This is because we should focus on our actual goal and desire, rather than the thing we're trying to get away from. It's hard to drive forward when you're only looking in the rear-view mirror.

It may seem elementary, but being able to check something off or erase an item from a to-do list has been proven to be an incredible tool in increasing productivity and serves as a satisfactory emotional reward.

Practicing 75/25

Living in alignment with our dreams also means providing space for them to grow. When we're working toward something we're passionate about, we may find ourselves bordering into the zone of overworking and, ultimately, impeding our progress. Oftentimes, you can look for signs in your environment when things start to get slow or when you suddenly have more free time than expected. This is typically an opportunity for you to take a break, spend time with loved ones, or look to some things that have been left on the back burner.

The rule of 75/25 is an idea where we spend 75 percent of our time working on our dreams—living in alignment and staying on track. The remaining 25 percent of the time is spent relaxing or doing other things. This could include having our Victory Meals, taking planned or spontaneous vacations, and even just lying on the couch with your pets. Practicing the rule of 75/25 gives us a chance to let things settle and work themselves out. If we spend too much time on our tasks, our mental and physical well-being will suffer, potentially leading to healthy challenges and other unwanted circumstances.

Remember Why

When we have a hard day (or week) our desires and intentions may start to get foggy. We start to forget the reason we've been inspired to be working so hard, and the opposing actions start to seem very enticing. In the element Quantum Delay, you'll be reading about cycles and how even our will power has a life cycle. This is why we have Victory Meals and rewards, but there is another tool that can help keep us in alignment. Write down a list of four or five reasons *why* you're working so hard. If you're trying to get healthier by changing your nutrition, then write a list of five reasons why you're doing it and keep it with you. Maybe it's to be a better role model to your children, to look good at your wedding, or to live a long, healthy life.

Whatever the reasons and whatever the intentions, write them down. In some cases all we need is a small reminder during our weak times to remember why we're doing what we're doing. You can keep this list in your pocket, in your car, on your bedroom mirror, or in front of the wine rack (that's right, I saw you). Put it wherever you usually end up when your inspiration starts to fade.

Personal Development

One of the easiest ways to begin to shift your alignment is through personal development. You've taken the first step by reading this book, and I hope you'll read others like it. Personal development doesn't stop at reading books, though.

Let's try to imagine again what we will be like when we live our dream life. Our future self will be more evolved and will have more skill and self-control than our current self. To become that, may need to redevelop aspects of who we *think* we are now to align with who it is we believe we can be. We need to be honest with ourselves about what needs to be worked on and actually work on it. Challenging yourself in ways that resonate with you will help strengthen your new emotional self and instill a confidence and courage to help you get through the hard times. This can include anything that challenges your body, mind, or soul to reach a higher level of your potential.

Some of my favorite avenues of exploration for personal development have been learning to become more sociable, challenging my physical stamina and strength, understanding business and finance, learning and composing music, exercising my intelligence and cognitive ability, learning new concepts about psychology and humanity and, of course, universal concepts and principles. Through challenging these aspects of my life, I've not only become a more confident and happy person, but I've also created new opportunities to share these ideas with others.

Personal development can mean anything from learning to pronounce words properly, improving your handwriting, or acquiring the skills to read body language from twenty feet away. Continually challenging ourselves makes us better at learning and better at adapting to challenging situations in life.

Emotional Alignment

Naturally, since our Emotional Self is the foundation of our ability to manifest, then it would serve as no surprise that our emotional alignment would also be something to be mindful of. Much like how our daily lifestyle choices and actions should be in alignment with our future self, so should our emotions. It's equally important to imagine how our future self will respond to emotional obstacles. Will the future you still have road rage? Will you get impatient when the line is too long at the grocery store? Will you get jealous over trivial or even seemingly big issues? Before you answer these questions, let's explore what these issues might mean.

Looking back at our old selves, it might make sense that we had road rage or impatience because, back then, we thought we were just unlucky or that others were jerks. We believed that we were victims and that crappy things *just happened* to us, rather than knowing that we were actually responsible for those things we experienced. Now we know that if someone is cutting us off in traffic, they could potentially be saving us from an accident up ahead. We know that although the grocery store line is long, we live a life of excitement and happiness, so this is a moment to relax and become present in the moment. We know that jealousy has no place in our lives because that is a fear-based emotion, and we are no longer prisoners of fear. We understand that confidence is not only attractive to others but attractive to *the universe* because it is a product of unquestionable belief.

We're going to cover this more in Quantum Delay, but being in alignment emotionally means *accepting* things we're currently experiencing because they are a manifestation of the past. We know that by accepting them, we're now believing and *knowing* that they are leading to our greatest desire. Can you believe that someone cutting you off in traffic is leading you to your greatest desire? I think you can. Has something ever happened to you that you huffed and puffed about only to shortly realize it presented an opportunity that couldn't have happened without it?

These opportunities present themselves constantly in our lives, but unfortunately, we spend most of our time resisting them before we get a chance to see their potential. Before long, we've created such an emotional turmoil that any potential opportunity that was there has shifted into inevitable turmoil. Take a breath, take a moment, observe the situation non-judgmentally, and imagine what the future you would do.

My Practice

Living in alignment is arguably one of the most important aspects of manifesting our dreams. All other aspects, for the most part, branch off from this. To this day, I continually find myself incrementally shifting my intentions and perspectives to steer myself in the direction of my desires. This is the type of practice that continually needs to be tended to. I use a Daily Dream Routine to keep me on track with meditation, exercise, writing, and many of my other important day-to-day activities. I also try my best to catch myself when I'm slipping into old patterns, and forgive myself when I've slipped more than I'm happy with. Much like steering a car or a boat, we need to continually make small adjustments to ensure we're moving in the most efficient direction. We want to strive for a balance of rigidness with adaptability.

Homework

Curious Creator – any 4   Master Manifestor – all

1) **Paint a picture.** Create a vivid mental picture of who you want to be in the future and write down those

traits. How will you eat? What will you drive? How will you treat others? Will you be happy? Will you be in a romantic relationship? Be specific.

2) **Create a routine.** Create a daily dream routine for your desires. Think of ways you can work toward your dreams everyday and write them on a list you can check off often (ie. exercise, meditate, drink 3L of water, write a gratitude list, etc). If you feel inclined, create a weekly or monthly routine, as well. We'll have a Daily Dream Routine app created for Android and iPhone posted at www.whataretheelements.com soon.

3) **Create a lifestyle budget.** Chart out a minimum and maximum style of living that is suitable to help you achieve your goals. Be sure not to limit yourself too much, but also keep it in alignment with your higher potential. Avoid using a dollar amount, but rather choose things like one coffee per day, one meal eating out per week, one movie night per week, etc.

4) **Read.** Always be working on a new personal development book, and try to read at least one new book per month. Follow your greatest excitement when reading them.

5) **Remember.** Write out a list of four or five points why you are making the changes you are. Perhaps it's to live a life of excitement, to become financially free, to help change the world, or to provide for your family. Write it down and look at it when you begin to fall out of alignment.

The only real valuable thing is intuition.

-Albert Einstein

ELEMENT 6

INTUITIVE FEEDBACK

Our hearts and minds are great tools for sending out messages and vibrations to the universe, but they also work great for receiving information. This information can come to us in a variety of ways such as a gut feeling, intuitive thought, or even a subtle voice in our head. In many beliefs, this is known as our intuition, sixth sense, higher self, or even as messages from the heart. How often has someone told you to listen to your heart? Perhaps they weren't that far off.

Oftentimes, people feel or experience these types of messages but mistake them as simply their own thoughts and sometimes doubt them. Our intuition *is* essentially coming from ourselves, as we are connected to the entire universe. Our core being feels these messages, and our mind interprets them in the best way it can, which often results in them appearing as simply thoughts, but maybe they're much more.

We can imagine our intuition (or higher self, or whatever you'd like to call it) as a travel guide standing at the top of a mountain, looking down on us trekking through a deep forest. From this higher point of view, our intuition can see the clearest and safest path for us to take, but since it's so far from us, it needs to yell loudly in order for us to hear it. Since it's so far away, the volume is still low by the time it reaches us, and if we're not listening intently, we may not get the message.

Our intuition is like our navigator or GPS system. It can help you see and understand the direction you're meant to go in and signals you when you're not. How many times have you done something that made you sick to your stomach or completely ashamed? That's also your intuition at work. You know, at the deepest level, who you really are. Your intuition is the communication system between your true self and the "you" that you believe yourself to be.

Listen, and Listen Again.

Sometimes we hear our intuition and get that gut feeling, but we're not sure if it's the right decision. We second guess it and start to create new, fabricated possibilities out of fear. Most of these possibilities are far from likely, but through using our imagination, we make that which we don't want much more likely to manifest. In moments like these, it's important for us to step back, take a couple of deep breaths, and try to look at the situation objectively. Most times, our emotions are so invested in a situation that we activate that fear mechanism, the amygdala, and it takes over our intelligent, intuitive mind. Try your best to take your own personal, invested emotions out of the equation for a moment and look at the situation objectively. This can be really tough to do, especially if the situation is very close to us. If necessary, ask a friend, counselor, or life coach to look at the situation. It's not that we can't hear our intuition; it's that we're thinking too loudly in the opposite direction to let it get through. It's always there, deep down, so try to silence the mind and give it a chance to speak up.

Mirror, Mirror on the Wall

A big part of Intuitive Feedback is the synchronistic reflection we can catch if we're sharp enough to see it. In The Shift, I talked about synchronicities and explained how they are often justified as coincidence or imagination. But what if the universe is directly sending us feedback about our subconscious mind affecting the reality around us?

Most of us have had the experience of thinking about someone then having them call or send a message at the same time, or maybe thinking about them and then seeing the exact type of car they drive. What about when you think of learning the guitar and you flip to a guitar lesson advertisement in the newspaper? I'm sure at least one of these examples sounds familiar. We've all experienced these and possibly even more profound types of "coincidences".

One of my practices for enticing the frequency and depth of synchronicities in my life is to try to write them down. I'll pick a specific topic in my life—a certain object I'm hoping to manifest or a person I'm looking to connect with. I'll write down each time I experience something I feel is significant, and I'll explain a few details about it. If I can't write them down, I'll mention it to someone in my Dream Team or even verbally acknowledge it to myself. Simply noticing these synchronicities will send out the intention that you want to experience more and are noticing them.

You might be wondering what the point or use of a synchronicity is. There are many beliefs surrounding them and whether they're something that happens by chance or something more mystical. I've done lots of research on them, from the scientific view to the metaphysical and spiritual aspect. Some believe that synchronicities are messages from angels or loved ones. Some think they might be messages from God or our souls. Many people believe they're just mathematical and psychological coincidences generated by sheer chance and awareness.

My personal belief, based on the information I've found, is that synchronicities are reflections of our internal intentions or strong vibrations, potentially even fears, actualizing in our reality. They are a reflection of our internal state being experienced in our external environment. In his book, *The Alchemist*, Paulo Coelho refers to synchronicities as omens and describes them as our "very own conversation with God". He mentions that your omens won't be the same as my omens, and we can be sure that they are a sign from the Language of The World.

Synchronicities might be perceived as the first physical manifestation of an idea. They're not quite formed enough to be the idea, but they might be a sort of embryonic experience. Maybe you're thinking about buying a new iPod next week, and then you see an advertisement for one online. Or maybe you're thinking about your dream car and a commercial comes on the radio about it. A few minutes later, you drive by the same style of car but in a color you don't really like...

Again, these events happen to us all the time, but we often just shrug them off, causing them to dissolve into the ether. Our external world is waving flags at us, showing us fragmented manifestations of our internal thoughts and desires, but we may seldom take notice. When these types of situations occur, I invite you to just take a short moment and take recognition. At least say to yourself, "hmm, look at that" and go on with your day. I promise you will start to notice more and more of these experiences.

Another explanation of synchronicities is the theory of pattern matching. Because we're looking for something, we take notice of it more so than other events, so it seems abnormal. Some doctors claim this is all a psychological phenomenon.

Dr. J.B. Rhine was a psychologist and researcher in the 1930s. During his practice, a man came into his office and claimed that he could influence the dice rolls with his mind. He couldn't control it all the time but enough to notice an effect. Rhine, obviously intrigued, told the man to show him. They took six pairs of dice, and the man was instructed to have the number six come up more than any others. The dice were tossed repeatedly, and to the doctor's surprise, it worked.

The chance over randomness averaged around 3 to 5 percent. Rhine repeated this experiment with coin throws, positions of objects when they land, and the rate of particle release from a radioactive source—they all came up the same. Though a seemingly small number, it was clear the effect was real. The act of observation and expectation *does* have an effect on the external universe.

To me, this presents two very interesting potential concepts that I have experienced plenty of times. First, it suggests that our internal state is projecting information onto our external state, visible for us to see, almost like a reflection. It also suggests that our expectation affects our external environment, meaning our internal state is influencing our external state... This suggests that maybe we can learn to tune in to our environment to watch the opportunities and intentions manifest. If you take notice of them and continue to expect them, you will eventually, little by little, manifest more of them in greater detail into your experience.

I know there are times in the book when things get deep and a lot of it may be hard to take in. I invite you to try to stay with me, give it a chance, and see it through to the end. You will find more and more value as you try to imagine these concepts and how they may be or have been present in your life. Try to have a child's mind with these ideas, and let your imagination soar. A persistent yet wild imagination is the most valuable asset we can have.

Dr. Kirby Surprise, author of the book *Synchronicity*, once explained that synchronistic events act like the mirror test on animals. Animals with higher intelligence recognize themselves in the mirror. Apes, humans, dolphins, and others can all recognize their own reflections. Synchronicities are much like this. The more aware and conscious we become, the more we can recognize our own reflection in our external environment.

When we expect others to behave a certain way, we are experiencing the reflection of that internal expectation externally in the world. When we expect our day to go great, we send out an image of a great day, and therefore, experience it. Synchronicities are the bright rays of the reflection that particularly stick out to us. They're the little breadcrumbs our subconscious mind is leaving for us to pick up so we can figure out where we're headed. If we use our navigational skills, we can use these experiences to guide us to a greater manifestation and to remind us of our creative abilities.

Avoid Distractions

In today's day and age, it's easy to become over stimulated and distracted. Our telephones have televisions, and we can watch people grow up from the other side of the world. We can become an expert at anything and visit anywhere on the planet with the click of a button. We know what's going on all across the world and which celebrities are making a scene in different cities. We know more about people we'll never meet than we do about the people we share the bus with.

It's very important to spend some time away from these distractions. Whether it's going camping for a weekend, sitting quietly while having coffee every day, or riding the bus without a book or music, it's important to give yourself time to think. Our culture is so full of gadgets, we have endless opportunities to be entertained, and everywhere we look, someone or something is trying to grab our attention, keeping us out of the conversation with ourselves.

Our intuition has the ability to speak to us about anything that we need, but we need to make sure we're listening. If our attention is wrapped up in the latest rock star meltdown or dramatic debates, we're going to miss its whisper and will continue to come up short.

I Spy With My Third Eye

We talk a bit about Extra Sensory Perception or ESP in The Shift, and I mention how, in the past century, some cool research has been done. People like Harold Sherman have dedicated most of their lives to experimenting, recording, and sharing data about the uses and potential benefits of ESP. Although more research may be needed, it seems apparent that humans have *extra senses* that sometimes defy logic or scientific explanation.

I wonder, though... Is it really that *out of this world* that we may have senses beyond our understanding and perception? Has anything like this ever been witnessed in nature outside of the human species? Most definitely. Birds have an internal, electromagnetic navigational system that helps them find their way across the world without ever having been to their destination before. Dolphins have an internal sonar system that navigates them through oceans for thousands of miles. Dogs can sense smells and sounds far beyond the human perception, and countless other animals have these so-called *instinctive* senses. Some may argue that animal instincts are no comparison to us exercising and cultivating extra senses, but is that really true? Dogs are trained to become better at using their sense of smell or sound. In fact, lots of animals are trained to use their various senses more accurately. Perhaps the question isn't whether or not we have these senses, but rather an inquisition into what these senses are and how we can strengthen them.

Harold Sherman describes a special technique he uses to strengthen his ESP and get him *in the zone,* so to speak. He says that to administer this technique, a person can lay on a couch or a bed and close their eyes. They should be wearing comfortable clothing and should put their attention on each part of their body until fully relaxing it. If thoughts come, they should simply observe them and let them go, focusing only on their breath. If I didn't know better, I'd say this sounds an awful lot like meditation...

And, of course, the technique Harold is describing *is* meditation. In The Now (at the end of the book), we talk about how practicing often can deprive our senses and help them become hyperaware, increasing the sensitivity of our sixth sense, also known as *intuition.*

Some people who claim to have an increased sense of intuition, or *psychic abilities*, might choose to use them for entertainment, such as fortune telling or readings. Others have used them to assist in police investigations, while many people simply use their increased sense of intuition to make better choices in their lives and to better connect with people through non-verbal communication. I personally don't believe that people *are* or *aren't* psychics, but rather that some people have developed and tuned their psychic abilities better than others. I believe we all have the potential to become more intuitive and to use our intuition for various intentions.

Some of us may be stronger in some areas than others or seem *naturally gifted* and talented, while some might need to work a bit harder. Regardless, we all have this sense, and strengthening it not only helps us make better decisions and connect with others, but it also sharpens our ability to interact with our environment and follow our path of greatest potential.

A Note for the Fortune-ate

As I mentioned above, a lot of highly intuitive people (also referred to as psychics) like to use their skills to offer services such as fortune telling or card reading. They might give advice on how you should change your life and warn you about future challenges or opportunities.

It's vitally important for each of us to remember that the future is *our* creation, not a creation from chance. When a fortune teller or psychic tells us information, it should be heeded simply as a suggestion on how to avoid or align with a *potential* future.

When we talk to someone who is highly intuitive, they will be empathetically picking up whatever is going on in our conscious mind. If we are anxious about an outcome, they will pick that up just as much as if we are excited about one. The information they receive will likely be in alignment with whatever is on our mind, and the suggestions or warnings they give will simply be a reflection of what we're thinking about. Ultimately it is *us* who creates the future with our expectations and beliefs. If you believe that something a psychic tells you is going to happen, then it is more likely to happen. Be sure to be very careful choosing what you're willing to believe as likely or simply pass off as not applicable.

Information from highly intuitive people can be very useful if used properly, so have fun with it and try to keep an open mind during your visit. A message from psychics is simply a form of channeled synchronicity.

Let Your Heart Sing

This is my favorite part about Intuitive Feedback. It's fun to talk about synchronicities and little signs from the universe, and it's intriguing to let our imagination run away with the ideas about a sixth sense, ESP, and the possibilities that come with it but, the really exciting part is when I talk about passion. Isn't that a hell of a word? *Passion.* Just saying it makes my heart flutter a little.

There are a lot of different ways to describe how to follow our passion. Paulo Coelho, in *The Alchemist*, calls it our *Personal Legend.* Some refer to it as a calling, a purpose, or simply doing what you love. Alan Watts approaches it with the rhetorical question, "What would you like to do if money were no object? How would you really enjoy spending your life?" To me, this might be the most important question in the world.

As I'm writing this chapter, I've recently started my fifth business. In terms of qualifications, I have no more than a community college education for business and a few years of sales experience to put on the table. The one asset I have that makes it possible for me to keep doing what I'm doing is passion. Now, I do have some passion for starting businesses. I happen to love the process of creating something from nothing. However, there are a couple of things that all of my businesses share. They're either created from monetizing something I truly love, or they solve a problem I feel I have the solution for. That's it. My passion is rooted in either the thing that I love or a problem I think needs to be solved.

For example, my most successful business right now is my nutrition coaching company, The Nutrition Blueprint. To become a nutrition coach, I took a one-thousand-dollar course marked down to two hundred dollars and started reading as many books on nutrition as I possibly could. I continued getting courses as I could and worked on my education both formally and informally. When I started, I decided that in-person coaching would take a lot of time, and I'd need an office, which I didn't have. Instead, I decided I'd create custom nutrition plans that allow people to eat better and get healthier and deliver them through email.

When I started the business, it took take me six to eight hours to create a plan, and I had a hard time getting people to pay for my services. To combat this, I worked my butt off, creating a system and formula to bring my per-plan time down to about an hour. After that, I started giving away as much information as I possibly could. I'd put on free seminars, write articles, offer free plans to people, give gift certificates to charities and more.

Before long, I was becoming well-known as somewhat of an authority on the subject, and people trusted me enough to pay me to coach them. In less than two years, I coached over four hundred clients worldwide with little advertising. It was definitely a necessity that I love nutrition, or I may have never collected the information I needed to create the system that was necessary for this success. Though I started with little formal education on the subject and basically no monetary investment, I *did* have the passion for the job. Every book or article I read and every video I watched, I thoroughly enjoyed. This business evolved because of my passion for nutrition and helping people.

Obviously, I like to take the entrepreneurial route to things and turn my passions into businesses, but that might not be for everyone, and that's ok. Following your passion and solving problems doesn't require you to open a business or even to do it as a career. The idea is to simply spend a little bit of time every day doing something that you truly love, something that really resonates with you.

What Do You Love?

Once in a while, when I'm discussing this concept with someone, they will come back and ask, "Well, what if I don't know what I love?" From the age of twelve, I remember following things that I love. Music was one of my first loves, starting with piano, but then moving on to guitar. Martial arts were next, with my training beginning in tae kwon do, then moving to karate, kickboxing, and eventually, mixed martial arts. Today, my heart is back with kickboxing. I've also had thirty-six jobs, twenty of them in sales, only to realize it's not selling for others I like. It's promoting products and services of my own that I'm passionate about that makes me most excited.

The thing is, finding what I love took me finding out a whole bunch of things I don't love. I spent a lot of time trying things out only to find out that my passion lies elsewhere. So when people ask me, "What if I don't know what I love?" I like to tell them to go out and find a whole bunch of things they don't love. By spending time trying things out and deciding which ones we like and which ones we don't, we're able to work with the contrast and become more effective creators.

The Key to Success

In North America and many parts of the world, it's commonly accepted that success is defined by the toys you own, the money in your bank account, and the clothes you wear, among other things. The thing I've found, though, is that most of the people who define success by these measures are continually chasing this illusion. Even when they get the toys, the clothes, and the money, they still don't *feel* successful. It seems they just want bigger toys, more clothes, and more money. So if success isn't measured by material things, then how can you possibly measure it?

Earl Nightingale wrote, "Success is the progressive realization of a worthy ideal". In other words, success is the day in, day out living in alignment with a purpose that is true to your heart. It's following your greatest excitement, offering the world your take on something, and finding enjoyment in the process itself. Have you noticed the word "money" in the past couple of sentences?

I like to think that success can easily be calculated by a simple formula: find something you love, get really, really good at it, and find a way to offer it to others. When I started nutrition coaching, I had no experience and no clients, so I offered to give all of my friends and family free nutrition plans just to gain some momentum. Before I knew it, people were emailing me from all over the world to get nutrition plans, costing me nothing in advertising. The trick is to get your work out there. Put your heart and soul into it. The money will follow. Maybe finding solutions to problems is what you love, so that can also fit into the equation. Whatever you love, use this formula. You will find yourself not only experiencing success, but also living a life of happiness.

Are You Happy?

In Vibratory Exchange, we talked about the difference between satisfaction and happiness. I'm the type of person that's rarely satisfied, however, the last time I truly felt unhappy is but a fleeting memory. I find my happiness in the process of finding satisfaction where there was once dissatisfaction. I truly enjoy the game of life, including the ups *and* downs. Happiness is not a place we get to. It's not some raise, promotion, vacation, or expensive purchase. It's the continual journey of solving problems, chasing excitement, and learning as we go. It's the cultivation of wisdom and collection of experiences. When I look back to where I've been from where I am now, I see attributes of success. I went from being homeless and jobless to enjoying all of the great things I've done in my life.

Success, for me, exists in hindsight. Do I feel successful as I write this book? Sure—more successful than I was yesterday and maybe not as successful as I will be tomorrow. Either way, the definition is not static; it's not something that's easy to define. Success is much like happiness; it's a journey that exists in relation to the particular position of a person's life now in relation to where it was at a point before.

Sometimes, we let others define things or answer our questions for us. Rather than look in the mirror and say, "damn I look good", we ask others how *they* think we look. If they don't toot our horn for us, we start to get insecure and worry. Worse still, if they confirm what we think, we often blush and start to argue with their opinion. Success works the same way. Do your best not to look to others for your measure of success or happiness. Try to let go of what the mainstream media and culture defines as "making it". Judge your success on how *you* feel. Do you wake up excited? Do you feel fortunate? Are you *happy?* If your answer is yes to any of these questions, then you, my friend, **are** successful. If your answer is no, then the next few paragraphs are for you.

Making It Happen

"And, when you want something, all *the universe conspires* in helping you to achieve it."

– Paulo Coelho

We talked about fear, right? We talked about how it's our primitive amgydala tricking us into thinking we're just talking monkeys on this Earth. That we're here through a procession of convenient events that mean nothing and that consciousness is simply a product of our physical brains. How it fools us into thinking our self-awareness is nothing more than phenomena like burping or farting. If I'm correct, we talked about how fear makes us dumb and sends us hurling away from our highest potential. Yeah, we talked about fear, so I'm going to ask you to remember that for the next few paragraphs.

I'm assuming (and hoping) that if you're reading this, you're an open-minded person. I believe it's safe to say that you don't always need scientifically proven evidence to take advantage of some of the universe's gifts, and if so, then you're going to be a few steps closer to manifesting your dreams.

Passion is rooted in the heart. For those who have been paying attention, that should say a lot. For those of you who haven't, I'll bring you up to speed: *our hearts are one of our greatest tools.* They help mold and form the world around us. When our desires and intentions are from the heart, the universe responds very quickly and effectively, bringing those dreams to life. Passion is a form of love, and love, of course, is the purest emotion, generated from the heart.

As Paulo Coelho mentions countless times in *The Alchemist*, along with most of the world's most successful people, when you combine passion with courage, *anything* is possible. The universe will bend at will. This doesn't mean you're going to instantly manifest your dream car into existence at the drop of a hat. It does mean you can start to incrementally shift into your passion, and through doing so, things like dream cars and dream houses will eventually *easily* manifest in relation to your happiness, and the easiest way to continually experience happiness is *passion.* Your soul aches for it, your heart *throbs* for it. Deep down, at the core of our very beings, what we all want is to wake up feeling excitement and passion for the day. Want to know the best part? The toys, money, and all of the rest will come as *products* of chasing our passion and living our greatest excitement. It's all complementary to living a journey of happiness.

The same goes for relationships. Do you know when you're most attractive? *When you're passionate.* I don't need to know you to know that. Passion is *the* most important ingredient in a relationship, both for the person we're in a relationship with and the things we do in our lives. If we're not chasing passion in our lives, then I'm afraid it may be a lonely road.

As I mentioned earlier, chasing your passion doesn't mean you need to start your own business. It doesn't mean you need to quit your job and move to Australia to surf or to ski in Banff. You do need to chase it, though, whatever it may be. If it's music you want to play start learning your instrument of choice. We live in a time where information is cheap and easy to come by. If you want to play music, then learn enough to play. It's that easy! If you want to save the world, then start looking for jobs that offer something that makes you feel like you're doing so.

If you want to spend most of your days on the be
working a full-time job, then start researching ho..
remotely and read books like *The 4 Hour Work Week*. Whatever
your passion is, whatever you would do if money was no object
you need to start doing it. There will be fear. There will be
circumstances that appear as failure, but I promise if you push
through and persevere, what you will find is the life you've
dreamed of. What you'll find is the treasure that is waiting for
each and every one of us.

The formula is easy: Passion + Action *despite* Fear = Limitless
Potential. When you take something that makes your heart sing,
pair it with execution, and proceed in spite of fear, *you will
make it happen.* Fear is like a parking brake. As long as it's in
control, we're not going to get far. Let it go and watch yourself
rise to heights you never thought possible.

My Practice

Learning to listen to our intuition is one of the most valuable
skills we can have. Knowing the difference between calculated
risk and submitting to fear can be the thing that takes you from
an ok life to a life beyond your wildest imagination. If you find
yourself absolutely terrified but your heart tells you to do it,
then you need to do it! If the opportunity screams potential but
your heart is telling you it's a bad idea, then you better well
listen.

My best practice for strengthening my intuition is to listen
closely. We'll be able to feel when something is wrong or right,
and the more we listen, the better we get at hearing it.

Meditation is a great way to clear the noise and static that fear and anxiety bring and will help us hone in on our true inner voice. The more I meditate, challenge my fears, and listen closely, the better I get at being a good listener. We all have the gift; the trick is just learning how to use it.

Homework

Curious Creator – any 3   Master Manifestor – all

1) **Find your passion.** If money was no object, what would you do in the world? What talent or passion would you share with others? Write this down in a paragraph or two.

2) **Reflect.** Keep a book or notepad with you or use your phone to record synchronicities you experience around you. What themes seem to be repeating themselves?

3) **Budget again.** Create a daily budget for how much time you spend watching television or browsing the internet. Your television limit should be much less than your internet limit, though both should be no more than a quarter of your time spent awake. I personally watch less than an hour or two of TV per week on average.

4) **Go for it.** Listen to your intuition, and do your best to face a new fear every day. Write this fear down in a journal and mention how you felt afterward and what you think it will do for you.

5) **Consult a psychic.** Sure, some may seem over the top, but I've been very fortunate to have consulted lots of incredible psychics who have truly helped my journey. Go see one. You might be surprised. Remember, if you expect it to be a waste of time, then it will be. Set your intention clearly before you go and have faith in the process. You determine the value of the experience.

6) **Open your eyes.** All three of them. Meditating, eating clean—humane and organic—drinking fluoride filtered water, and other practices mentioned in Emotional Self will help you open your third eye more and increase your intuition. Do your best to practice these things daily.

"Faithless is he that says farewell when the road darkens."

-J. R. R. Tolkien

ELEMENT 7

QUANTUM DELAY

We've learned how to prepare our mind and body to become a foundation for manifestation in the first two elements. After that, we learned how to become mindful about our exchange of vibrations with the world around us, and we learned how to paint the picture of the reality we want to experience. We learned how to align our lives with that reality and how to listen to cues and hints on where we're going and what to do next. Many of you may already be experiencing some of the miracles I've mentioned in this book, and some of you may still be waiting. Some of you might even be getting a little bit impatient with your results and wondering, "Where's mine?" That's what this chapter is about.

In short, this chapter is about the time between your intention for an experience and the actual manifestation of the experience itself. We'll explore why some things might take longer than others and the types of obstacles you may face in the meantime. We'll talk about some of the tricks and tools you can use while waiting for your desire and also some of the mistakes made in between.

There's a vicious cycle that happens in this game of manifestation. Most people, me included, will be on a roll with being mindful of their thoughts and actions, working toward easily manifesting their dreams, then will hit a wall. Impatience will kick in, and before we know it, we've slipped back into the old patterns again, thinking negatively and doubting this whole process. This is all too common but can easily be avoided with some discipline.

Again, we go back to the seed I talked about in Vibratory Exchange. Imagine for a moment that you've planted a seed in your garden. For a day or two, you're excited and can't wait to see what magic will come out of the soil. A few days pass, though, and you start to get impatient. One morning, you go out to the garden and dig up the seed. You see a little bud sprouting, but you start to doubt the time it's taken so far. You start to wonder if this time frame is normal and if maybe something's wrong.

The next day, you wake up and do the same thing and notice that nothing has changed. Getting more frustrated, you dig the seed up day after day, and before long, what was somewhat sprouted has shriveled up and died. The plant that had all of the potential in the world is now damaged and destroyed. Your attachment to the outcome based on a time frame *you* created in your mind has caused you to destroy what could have been a healthy, vibrant creation. Now you've formed new beliefs and doubts about your ability as a gardener and either repeat the entire vicious cycle again or fail to even bother trying.

Does this sound familiar? I know I've been through this many times in my past. Our desperate attachment to a present outcome acts as a barrier to our desire actualizing into our experience. We think because we're not experiencing what we want *now*, then maybe it's not going to happen at all. We get angry and frustrated, bringing ourselves into a destructive frequency, which only manifests more of this experience and an outcome we don't want. The fear of our desire not manifesting acts as a parking brake, limiting the potential of the experience to happen in a timely manner to its fullest extent, if it even happens at all.

This is the vicious cycle of impatience that is very present in our culture. We want everything now, now, now, and when we don't get it, we throw fits and tantrums. Rather than settle into the moment, enjoying the process of creation, we fabricate worries about the future and doubt its possibility. Esther Hicks once said, "Can you imagine the absence of satisfaction that a sculptor would have if in the moment he touched the clay it just became the statue?" What enjoyment would there be? How could he feel proud of his work?

Unfortunately, there is no way for us to determine *how long* it will take for a desire to manifest. However, the good news is as you become a better, more experienced creator, the manifestation time can get incredibly fast. I've manifested experiences into my life on some occasions that have left me in awe for days. I've watched friends who are also powerful creators talk about something one day and see it materialize the next. It brings with it an incredible feeling of empowerment and freedom.

Let It Go

One of the most important yet most challenging aspects of Quantum Delay is letting go of our expectation of how we *think* a situation is going to manifest into our experience. Deepak Chopra calls this concept "the law of detachment". The basic idea is that once we've clearly sent our intentions for what we want out into the universe, we need to just detach from that desire and go on with our day. Simple, right? I didn't think so, at least, not at first.

When it comes to manifesting a free parking spot or some extra Air Miles I wasn't expecting, then sure, detachment, no problem. But what about when it comes to getting the mortgage paid on time? What about having enough for the car insurance this month? How do we detach from that?

Well, that's just it. We don't, not really. The idea isn't to completely detach from something we desire; that's nearly impossible. The idea is to let go of the *expected outcome* of a situation and to understand that the *current situation* is simply just that—the current situation. It does not determine or dictate what the coming situations and experiences will be. Just because you don't have the mortgage payment *today* doesn't mean you can't or won't tomorrow.

As human beings, we tend to carry this arrogance that we are able to predict how a situation is going to transpire. We (or at least I) tend to perform immense, intricate mental calculations about how this is going to turn into that and how we're going to get from point A to point B. This is one of the symptoms of the *monkey mind* often referred to in the context of meditation. Unfortunately, manifestation is not something we can ever fully understand, and the universe has aspects of the formula and abilities to create circumstances we can't perceive.

The obsessive, compulsive need to know *how* something is going to happen and the anxious, petrifying fear we experience while it's not showing up in our experience is *attachment.* This is a dangerous, destructive emotional state that displays total lack of faith in our abilities as creators and in the ability for the universe to present miraculous circumstances beyond our scope of understanding. In this state, we are giving in to our primitive fear-based intelligence and often do more harm than good.

This isn't to say that your desires *can't* manifest when living in this state. Sometimes they can, but if so, it's usually only partially manifested and/or significantly delayed. Attachment is another parking brake.

Your Presence is a Present

So I assume you're wondering, *how do I practice detachment?* Great question. The first way is easy, and if you haven't guessed it already, it's meditation. Meditating daily is a fantastic tool for taking us out of the guilty past and fearful future by bringing us back to the present moment. The best part is regular meditation will allow us to stay in the present moment, even when we're not meditating, and will also help relieve the anxiety of attachment throughout our daily lives. Meditation enhances the neuroplasticity of our brains and strengthens the wiring that lends to confidence, calmness, compassion, and faith. Have you started meditating yet?

The second method is actually easier than the first and is something anyone can practice—be excited. No really, it's that simple. Following our excitement is by far *the* quickest way to practice detachment and speed up our manifestation time. Now, I don't expect you to sit around proclaiming, "No money? Who cares! Woo hoo!" However, while you're waiting for your bills to get paid, the new raise at work, or an amazing person to keep you breathless, you can follow other aspects of your life that keep you excited. Do you like to paint? Then paint! Do you like to exercise? Get moving! Do things that make you excited and keep you out of sitting around sulking about the thing you want that hasn't appeared yet.

Stay Happy

If your desire is to be a famous dancer, then dancing may be one of the things that make you excited. If so, then do lots of it. However, if your desire to be a famous dancer is so strong that you start to find yourself almost obsessing about dancing out of fear that your desire won't manifest, then it might be a better idea to try something else. There is a fine line between dedication and determination versus an unhealthy obsession. As a nutrition coach, I have come across far too many people obsessing about their physical appearance, so much so that even when they hit their desired goal, they can't enjoy it. In some cases, they're almost unable to see their changes and remain unhappy despite their obvious progress. They've created an unhealthy level of dissatisfaction rather than a level that drives them to excel and reach their highest potential. Typically, these types of attachments to a desire run much deeper than the desire itself and are about something much more complex. It's important for us to be honest about *why* we have a certain desire and what it means to us to manifest it. Ask yourself the question, "Will I be happy *as* I manifest this goal?" If your answer isn't "yes", then perhaps there's a bit more work to be done first. Remember, happiness is a journey, not a superficial destination. It's quite simply a state of mind generated from within. Are you happy? Whatever the answer, you'll find it inside.

Spotting the Blocks

Much like a long road trip across the country, the journey of manifesting our dreams can also have some detours and road blocks. It's very important for us to know when we need to go around or *through* a barrier on the road ahead. I'll give you an easy example that I've come across in my coaching career. When money would get tight I'd often find myself only focusing on the aspects of my job that were most profitable and would leave the less or unprofitable aspects "until later". This might include cleaning my office, creating free nutrition plans I promised to give away, doing volunteer work, or other tasks I was already committed to.

I quickly realized there was a trend that was happening when I would leave the smaller things for too long; everything would just come to a stop. It became inherently clear to me that the universe was only going to send me what I could handle. If I wanted more profitable tasks like new clients or side jobs, I needed to get the other stuff on my to-do list out of the way first. Sure enough, once I cleared most of my to-do list, the work and opportunities would start pouring in.

The same concept can be applied to having gratitude for the smaller things we're experiencing. If we don't appreciate the small gifts the universe sends us because we're too attached to the bigger desire, then it's not very likely it's going to come in a timely manner. It's important to remember to practice our vibratory exchange. If we're not keeping ourselves in a high vibration, then it's going to be nearly impossible to manifest something that exists in that frequency.

When we find ourselves facing more blocks than usual, there may be value in going back to the foundation of our mind and body by asking ourselves what type of language we're using, what type of daily activities we might be cutting corners with, or how we're treating other people. The answer to what's holding us back can always be found with a little bit of introspection.

To ensure we have a clear road ahead in our journey, it's important to be honest with ourselves about what type of work we have to complete, what type of attachment we're applying to the desire, and what other personal development we may want to work on in the meantime. It's easy to get caught up in our emotions and place the blame externally for why a desire isn't actualizing, but with a little bit of self-honesty and insight, we can remove the blocks and get back to smooth sailing.

Contrast Questions

There have been countless times I've found myself experiencing contrast that seemed a little outside of the norm. Maybe business would get really slow, or bills would start piling up without much money coming in. Challenging obstacles would pop up out of nowhere, and things would seem a little more difficult than usual. In these times, I ask myself some Contrast Questions. Contrast Questions are self-inquiries that may help me determine areas in my practice I may be overlooking or neglecting. My favorite contrast questions are:

- Have I been volunteering?

- Have I been donating?

- Have I been living in alignment?

- Have I been competing all of my tasks?

- Have I been getting sufficient rest?

- Have I been practicing presence and mindfulness?

The answers to these questions almost always offer some insight about what I may have been missing. Perhaps I've been overworking, focusing only on monetary tasks rather than enjoyment, neglecting my volunteering, or acting out of alignment. If you think you've experienced this, try making a list of questions that can help bring you back into the direction of your dreams. When you find yourself experiencing contrast, read them through. The answers you're looking for might have been there all along.

Round and Round We Go

What goes up must come down... It's always darkest before dawn... There's light at the end of the tunnel... It's always calm before the storm... Sound familiar? After day comes night, after winter comes summer, and after too much wine comes the inevitable wine hangover. Everything in nature has a cycle, so why would we think good fortune would be any different?

We may sometimes find ourselves moving smoothly in the flow of manifestation, with everything going right, only to hit a wall. It seems nothing could go wrong, then out of nowhere, anything that can go wrong, does. It's during these times that our abilities to manifest are most effective, though, and most crucial. How we react will determine the duration of contrast that we experience, as well as the potential of the good times to come. We might try to remember that it's the contrast that reminds us of what we don't want and sends us in the direction of what we do. When we use contrast as a tool, we really enhance our experience. It's our reaction in the valleys that determines the height of our peaks.

Having the ability to manifest our desires doesn't mean it's never a challenge or doesn't get slow. There has to be a balance in the universe; this is one of the most fundamental laws of nature. Everything must balance. Your valleys might not have to be as low as they once were, and your peaks may reach new heights, but there *must* be a cycle; it's just the nature of nature.

Whether or not we experience a valley as *negative* or *positive* is our choice, however. You might be thinking, "I don't choose to experience negative circumstances!" and that may be true, though you *do* choose, or at least accept to *perceive* them as negative. Remember that jerk that cut you off? Was that really a negative situation, or was he saving you from a potential wreck up ahead? How can you possibly know? You can't, of course, but you can choose to give these situations in your life the benefit of the doubt. There's no question that you were cut off, that we can agree on, but whether or not it was a good or bad thing is yet to be determined, so why bother letting yourself get worked up about it?

I attended a presentation at Dalhousie University in Halifax featuring Buddhist Monk, Ajahn Brahm, where he told a story that offers some insight into our choice to see something as good or bad. The story was about a King many hundreds of years ago who hunted, often on horseback. He brought his physician so if anything happened, he could get immediate medical attention. Once, while on a hunting expedition, he injured a finger while hunting a bore. In a frantic, he asked the physician "Is it bad?" To which the physician responded, "Good, bad, who knows?" The King irritated and in a panic, had the physician sew the wound and told him that he'd better hope, for the sake of his freedom, that the wound would heal.

A week went by, the finger became infected, and the physician had to amputate it. The King, furious, screamed at the medic and said, "You told me this would be fine!" The physician said, "Your highness, I told you good, bad, who knows?" On a rampage the king threw the physician into the dungeon to stay for the rest of his days.

A month or so later, the King went on another hunting expedition and was kidnapped by some local natives who had the intention to sacrifice him. They brought the King back to their village and quickly realized who they had captured. These natives usually sacrificed animals to their Gods, but now they had caught a King! Surely their gods would be ecstatic.

They tied the king to a tree and started their ceremony. With drums pounding, each of them chanting in their native tongue, they prepared to slit the throat of the King, but just before they did, one of the natives realized he was missing a finger. "We can't give him to our Gods, he's deformed; that would be disrespectful! The Gods would be furious!" Disappointed, the natives cut the King loose and sent him on his way.

The King returned to the castle and hurried down to the dungeon to free the physician from his shackles. "I am so embarrassed. I locked you up out of anger only to find out it is because of you that I am still alive, I am sorry." The physician said, "Your highness, I told you, good, bad, who knows!" Puzzled, the King responded, "How can this be good? You've been locked away all this time! I took away your freedom for nothing." But the physician smiled, held up his hands, and said, "Yes, but I have all of my fingers. If you hadn't locked me up, I would have been the one who was sacrificed! That is why I say good, bad, who knows!"

All too often, we are too emotionally invested in a situation to be able to look at things from the outside in. While in the heat of the moment, it's difficult for us to actually see the potential possibilities that arise from a seemingly negative situation because we simply aren't aware of them. Our only choice is to trust that they are there and watch them manifest.

These cycles I'm explaining shouldn't be viewed like a circle. If that were the case, then it would imply that we are stuck in the same continual experience of ups and downs. Rather, we should imagine it like a gradually inclining wave. The highs get higher than ever before, and the lows are never quite as low as they once were. This happens because we are more intelligent, more resourceful, and more *evolved* than we've ever been before. We're more capable of dealing with challenges because we have the experience needed to do so. Our awareness and consciousness has expanded beyond the scopes of what we've had in previous encounters of a seemingly similar situation.

Let me give you an example. Imagine for a moment that you've actually never learned how to read. When you look at words and sentences, all you see are shapes that you can't comprehend. Now imagine that you've suddenly learned how to read. The shapes that once meant nothing now explode with information. Your awareness and consciousness of their meaning and what they represent has expanded. This same concept can be applied to *everything* in life. The more experienced and wise we become, the more we're able to tackle situations that were once too challenging. Through experience, we evolve.

The Darker Cycles

When I talk about this concept of cycles, I get asked questions like, "Well, what good comes from an economic crash?" or "What about the high levels of homeless people in North America?" I don't have an easy answer. There is a lot of pain that exists in life that we have no explanation for. If I had to give an answer, though, I might say that with every economic downfall comes an influx of new business owners giving up on the nine-to-five job they never really liked in order to chase their dream—whatever it is—because what do they have to lose?

I might say that the high levels of homeless and needy people are opportunities for each of us to take the initiative and make a difference from the ground up. I might even say that some of the worst events in history, once resolved, have inevitably brought our species closer together than ever before. If I had to answer, I'd say it is these dark times which force us to break down the barriers between each other and to remember that we're all in this together.

Will I?

One of the most important yet undermined cycles is that of willpower. As a wellness coach, I know how important willpower is for the success of any goal we set. Without willpower, few of us will ever see even a hint of accomplishment, let alone all of our wildest dreams. But what do we do when our willpower crumbles? How do we deal with temptations and desires that overcome us? First, let's try to understand what willpower is.

Willpower is essentially a term that explains our ability to focus and follow through on a goal or accomplishment from the time of conceiving it to actually achieving it. Whether it's to fit into a wedding dress, perform a muscle up, run a marathon, or save up for a new pair of shoes, it takes willpower to get from *wanting* to do it to actually doing it. With this in consideration, we might say that willpower is the forward driving force that helps us get from here to there.

We're going to use our imagination for a moment again. Let's say your desire is to look good on the beach when you go away on vacation in a couple of months, and to do so, you have to stick to a regular fitness routine and eat healthy. You find yourself going one week, two weeks, maybe even three, but then you crash. You've made it to the gym every day for weeks and never stray from the diet, but then the pressure is too much and you crack. You sit home all weekend eating nothing but pizza, cookies, and ice cream. Monday rolls around, and you feel so guilty and depressed that you let yourself down; all you want to do is sleep. A few days go by, you haven't made it to the gym, and you can't bring yourself to prepare your food for the week. Bit by bit, you slip back into your old habits of not working out and eating garbage.

Or maybe you've been saving up for a new car. You've given up your five-dollar lattes every morning and have stopped eating out, but after a week or so, you just want to relax. You're tired of cooking all of your food at home and missing out on drinks with friends, so finally, for lack of better judgment, you go out with friends and end up spending two hundred dollars, most of which, you can't even remember spending.

In both of these situations, we have a clear case of broken willpower. You've worked your butt off, stayed on track as long as you could, but finally, you have just crashed. The pressure of avoiding temptation has gotten the better of you. Most of us have experienced this kind of cycle at one time or another in our lives. The issue here isn't your willpower. In fact, your willpower is likely no better or worse than mine or anyone else's. The issue here is the understanding of how willpower works and how we can maximize its efficiency and effectiveness.

Some people have an impeccable ability to stay on track for weeks, months, and even years when it comes to a goal or desire. They're able to keep their eye on the prize under all circumstances and do what needs to be done to reach their goal, no exceptions. These people might include Olympic athletes, world famous musicians, or other almost superhuman individuals. Despite their obvious success, most of these people have a very high burn out rate. They can maintain this level of output for a few years, and then might spontaneously crack under the pressure. Some may even suffer from obsessive compulsive disorder and other psychological issues that spawn out of this kind of pressure. The unrealistic expectations they've put on themselves have drained the enjoyment and love out of the journey they're on to work toward what they're looking to achieve.

Willpower, like most processes in nature, has a cycle. After so long, the majority of us not only deserve but *need* a break from the pressure of working on our goal. We have to take some time to regroup, mentally and physically, so that we can realign ourselves and stay excited about what it is we're looking to achieve. If you're looking to drop a few pounds before a vacation, then scheduling a weekly Victory Meal to celebrate your hard work is a great way to rev up the willpower again. Setting a realistic budget that allows you to spend a little bit here and there will make it easier to save for that big purchase. Create a scheduled "willpower break" that allows you to slip up purposely in order to reward yourself for your hard work. In the end, not only will you reach your goal, but you'll do so much quicker and be happier.

Remember to Dance

I really believe that dancing is a sort of mythical and magical practice that everyone needs to partake in. I don't just mean breaking it down at the staff party or jumping on stage at a concert, though those of those are fun, too. I mean understanding that all of our daily actions, conversations, challenges, relationships, and anything we do can be viewed as our part in the dance of life. Every time we speak to someone, we are either listening intently or waiting for our own opportunity to talk. When we're driving in rush hour, we're either completely consumed by where *we* need to go, or we're letting others in because maybe their time is valuable, too. When the bills are due, we're either feeling grateful that we even have services that require bills, or we're pulling our hair out worrying about how they're going to get paid. There is a dance to this thing called life, and whether we choose to move with it or against it will be what determines our enjoyment or our suffering. If we eat a little bit slower, listen a little bit better, and try to be both a leader *and* a follower, we might find ourselves swaying and moving to the beautiful music that is there for us to hear.

Meditation for Manifestation

I mention meditation a lot in this book, and the next chapter tells most of what I know about it. As you probably realize by now, our ability to effectively manifest our dreams is a balance of emotional, physical, and spiritual health. When I say spiritual, I don't necessary mean religious, though I don't exclude it, either. Spiritual, to me, means our connection to others, our connection to our environment, and our connection to the universe.

During meditation, we are transcending our conscious mind, bringing ourselves below the chitter chatter of the brain and working to exist beneath all of the psychological ideas we have about ourselves. In other words, we are transcending the *ego*. We bring ourselves into connection with our true self.

The benefits of meditation are endless and include all of the great stuff I've mention earlier and touch on again in The Now, including relieving our stress, worry, fear, insecurities, and much more. By removing these mental patterns, we are able to more effectively shift into alignment with our dreams and have those dreams manifested into our lives. Fear is the ultimate parking brake, so when we change our belief about a fear or move forward despite it, we are letting that parking brake go. We are reaching a higher level potential.

When it comes to the law of attraction or quantum shifting (which you'll learn about shortly), meditation actually acts like a clutch, allowing our manifestations to form out of pure potential. When we're continually thinking about our dreams and almost obsessing about whether or not they're going to manifest, we're almost remaining *too* attached to them, limiting their potential. Following our excitement, practicing meditation in motion, like yoga or dance, or staying in a high vibration can help us shift to that reality, but nothing is more effective than meditation.

When we meditate, we step out of the reality we're looking to shift from and sit in a state of pure potential, beginning our incremental shift into the reality in which we do want. Meditation is the clutch which shifts us into the life of our dreams. If we are ever looking for a dream to manifest faster, meditation is the way to achieve that.

My Practice

Finding peace in the delay between intention and manifestation is a continual challenge for even the strong at heart. I won't say it ever gets *easy*, but through staying excited, chasing our happiness, practicing acceptance, and resisting little, we can find the flow that gets us from where we are to where we want to be. It still takes hard work and an ability to see things for what they are. The more we remember this, the richer our manifestations will become.

My best practices for working with the Quantum Delay have been through continually reminding myself to stay present in the moment and trusting that the current circumstances are simply a manifestation of my thoughts and intentions in my past. Sometimes, I can see the lessons and opportunities unfolding in front of me as I'm experiencing delay and contrast, while other times, they remain hidden until the right time. One thing I can always count on is that when the dust settles, there is a hidden gem waiting for me beneath it all.

Remember, there are no good or bad experiences, just experiences. Whether we perceive them to be good or bad is a choice, and it is up to us to decide how we'd like them to turn out. We have a very powerful ability within us, and when we find it, our lives will change forever.

Homework

Curious Creator – any 3   Master Manifestor – all

1) **Take a break.** Schedule yourself willpower breaks and downtime when planning for your goals. Being overworked will only lead to burn out and, ultimately, falling short of your goal.

2) **Dance.** Each time you come to a challenge, write down three ways that it could potentially lead you to something better. Be creative! When you imagine these possibilities, you create them. Learn to dance with your challenging situations.

3) **Write your contrast questions.** Write out a number of questions you can ask yourself when you're experiencing contrast, and read them whenever you need to.

4) **Name the blocks.** Name three blocks that are standing in the way of your current manifestations, and name how you will change them. Next step: change them! Start working on this right away.

5) **Take a moment.** Each time you face contrast, take a few breaths and bring yourself back to the present moment. When you feel more grounded, go back to the situation.

THE NOW

MINDFULNESS AND MEDITATION

When I originally started writing this book, I was planning on talking about meditation just briefly within a few chapters. However, I realized that it's been too significant in my life to mention it only slightly, so I've decided to feature a chapter on it.

Like many aspects of this book, meditation is not necessarily *obligated* for success in realizing our dreams. However, it is an incredibly useful tool that as you will learn, can speed up the progress substantially. I like to think of meditation as jet fuel for dreamscaping.

Perhaps, as you're reading this book, you'll find that meditation isn't something you're interested in trying, and that's ok. I'm still going to suggest you read through this chapter because it will give you some useful information that you can reference should you ever decide to try meditation out.

Before I talk about meditation, I want to explain the idea of mindfulness. Mindfulness can be understood as simply being present in the moment. Author Eckhart Tolle wrote an entire book on this concept called *The Power of Now*. He refers to it as *presence* versus mindfulness, but the idea is the same. When we practice mindfulness, we are becoming present in the moment, not worrying about the future or the past. A simple way to jump into a state of mindfulness is to become aware of a part of our body. If you *feel* your toes right now, chances are you aren't thinking of any thoughts at the same time. This is mindfulness. Another way to jump into a state of mindfulness is to think of the first thought that comes to your mind. Ready? Go.

Did you have a moment without a thought? If so, this is also a state of mindfulness. Meditation might be understood as the practice of continued mindfulness or the practice of presence. The idea is to become presently aware of our current state of self and stay there for a moment. The technique is called "practicing" meditation because there is no destination to get to; it is the practice itself that is the achievement. The idea is not to be the "best" at meditation, but rather to find enjoyment in the practice for the sake of practicing.

There are a lot of styles of meditation that have their roots in many different places, including various religions and cultures. However, I'm going to keep it very simple and stick to the basics. If you're looking to find out more about meditation, there are endless resources online and in your city; it just takes a bit of looking around.

The meditation I currently practice is a style called insight meditation, or "vipassana", which means "to see things as they really are". This style of meditation is one of the most widely practiced and simple forms of meditation out there, however, it's not the style I started with.

I tried to learn to meditate many times unsuccessfully until eventually seeking an instructor. I found an instructor of Transcendental Meditation, which is a style that has become very popular in North America because of its easy-to-learn method. Transcendental Meditation, or TM, is a style of meditation that uses a *mantra*—a word repeated to aid in concentration. The mantra is given to you by your instructor, and you're not supposed to tell it to anyone or it may lose its significance (apparently). TM can be practiced sitting on the floor or in a chair and is intended to be practiced twice a day, in the morning and the evening, no less or more than fifteen to twenty-five minutes.

TM was definitely an effective method of learning meditation, but it came at a price—a little over fifteen hundred dollars for a four-day course. I admit that I did learn how to meditate from the course. However, now that I've learned so many other methods and styles, including becoming an instructor of vipassana, I realize that paying such a high price is—in my opinion—absurd. I think everyone should have the ability to learn meditation for an affordable price, if not free, as it is so beneficial to them and everyone around them. This belief lead me to become a meditation instructor and bring the teaching to anyone who was willing to learn.

Before I get into the "how to" of meditation, I want to briefly explain some of the benefits. In a hard facts sense, meditation has been proven to decrease stress and anxiety, increase compassion, lower blood pressure, reduce and even reverse depression, and alleviate addiction withdrawal symptoms. It increases serotonin—the feel-good hormone—improves the immune system, and increases energy. Basically, it makes you a healthier, happier human in a plethora of ways.

In terms of dreamscaping, it helps you realize who you really are: a powerful creator. Meditation will challenge your limiting beliefs, help you overcome your fears, and give you the courage to follow whatever dreams you can conceive. It will clear out the mental junk you have holding you back from reaching your highest potential and helps you shift your reality into whatever you choose. It increases your intuition, instills patience and acceptance, as well as a love and respect for others around you. Meditation has been proven to actually change the plasticity of your brain, quite literally upgrading you as a human being. It increases intelligence, neural cognition, memory, creativity, focus, and so much more. I could fill pages with the benefits of meditation, but I think you get the idea.

The hardest part about learning to meditate was all of the misconceptions I had about it. As far as I knew, meditation meant that you sit for a period of time without thinking. Sounds easy, right? Not so much. I would try over and over to "not think", only to be bombarded even further with more thoughts. In fact, I don't really remember more than a moment going by *without* a thought. There was no way in the world I was going to be able to learn to meditate. That is, until I learned that "not thinking" is not what meditating is about.

As it turns out, even some of the most experienced meditation practitioners in the world have about ten thoughts per minute. Thinking is inevitable, everyone does it. There are two terms used in meditation to refer to the actions of our mind: "thinking" and "sinking". The thinking mind is pretty simple; it's full of thoughts. The sinking mind, on the other hand, is basically that moment right before you're about to fall asleep and is not much better than not meditating at all.

So thinking is normal? Well yes, but it's a bit more complicated. *Thoughts* are a part of meditation, but *thinking* shouldn't be. You see, thoughts are part of our mind and are bound to happen, whether we like it or not. What we do next is what matters. We can think the thought, or as I call it "follow the rabbit", and elaborate on all of the details. The thought might be "I need to do the dishes", with the succeeding thoughts being "how many dishes are there?" and "will I have time?" or "I wonder what's for supper? This is what I mean by following the rabbit.

The other option is to *observe and release* the thought. So again, the thought "I need to do the dishes" comes into your conscious mind, but you choose to stop it in its tracks and maybe think "not now", going back to focusing on your breath. You observe the thought like a cloud passing by on a sunny day and go back to focusing on your breath.

At first, it might seem that the thoughts are coming repeatedly, and they likely are. When we begin as new meditation practitioners, we have a lot of mental "junk" in our minds. It's sort of like storm clouds, distracting us from focusing on our breath. As we practice meditation more often, the junk starts to clear, and we begin to find some peace behind it all. The problem is that it takes time, and most people give up long before they reach this state. Trust me. From experience, it will come. In my experience, both personally and teaching, anyone hoping to learn to meditate should commit to at least fourteen days. It takes time to form a new habit, and sometimes, they don't come easy. I use this same formula for exercise, nutrition, and any type of lifestyle change. If you're really determined, you can take the twenty-eight days of meditation challenge, which I explain at the end of this chapter.

So once I figured out how thoughts worked, I still had some other confusion. How do I sit? How do I breathe? Does it matter? First of all, the breathing part is easy; simply breathe in and out of your nose in a consistent manner, filling up your belly and letting it all out. I like to take a few deep breaths in my nose and out of my mouth to get started and to fill the body with oxygen. I also like use my meditation as an opportunity for deep breathing exercises, so I breathe deeply into my belly. If more shallow breaths feel natural to you, then that's ok, too.

Postures of Meditation

In my opinion, the best posture for meditation is one that allows you to focus on your breath without significant pain. It's important to be honest with yourself about discomfort, which can bring discipline and potential injury, which can be dangerous. Posture can be a tool when used properly.

There are three levels I break postures into. The first level is simply sitting in a chair with your spine upright or on the floor with your back leaning on something. This will give you support while you sit. The next level would be sitting on a cushion or chair without your back actually touching anything. This will help you start to build the muscles in your trunk and lower back to support your posture. Your back is still aligned properly with the natural curve. This allows you to fully breathe deeply and make sure you're getting enough oxygen.

Finally, level three postures are sitting with your pelvis elevated slightly higher than your knees without your back touching anything. This is best achieved with a meditation cushion or block. You may have to play around to find what works best. You can sit cross-legged or in two traditional meditation postures called half lotus and full lotus. I personally have big legs, so I sit on two cushions in a half lotus position.

Meditation is the cultivation of self-awareness and can be practiced by simply being aware of the self behind the thoughts—the observer. It's a combination of concentrating and being mindful at the same time, a balance of resilience and flexibility. I believe that a person can get lots of benefits from meditation simply by sitting in a chair and keeping it simple, so find what works for you. The important thing is to find something you can stick to.

Meditating While Laying

Some people enjoy practicing meditation while lying down. According to TM, this is not suggested because it makes it easy for the subject to fall asleep. I personally don't fall asleep easily, but someone who does may want to stick to sitting meditation. There are some methods of meditation, which I'll cover shortly, that in my opinion are best while lying down, but sitting is suitable for basic insight or vipassana meditation.

Methods of Meditation

I mentioned earlier than there are different styles of meditation, and I'm not going to really dive too much into them, but in general, I want to cover four specific methods I use in my practice. The first two methods are derivatives of insight/vipassana meditation that I call intention meditation and visualization meditation.

Intention meditation is the practice of simply focusing on the breath and being present in the moment. I call it intention meditation because I like to create an intention for the meditation, such as something I wish to manifest or someone I'm thinking about. Maybe the intention is simply to be free of stress or to relax. Either way, it doesn't mean I *think* about the desire, it simply means I sent that intention *before* the meditation. During the meditation, I simply focus on the breath or use a focus technique.

In this method, we're observing thoughts and releasing them. This type of meditation is the one I suggest that everyone practice at least once per day, preferably in the morning. This method is the one I refer to as "manifestation jet fuel". It clears out that mental junk and offers all of the incredible benefits I mentioned earlier. This should be the real pillar of your meditation practice with the following methods being secondary.

Visualization meditation is a method that is usually specific to a goal or desire you're looking to manifest. Basically, the subject will start their first five to ten minutes with presence meditation then shift to a vivid visualization of their desire. Athletes will use this to visualize their sport, and others may visualize a presentation, sales pitch, or anything that may require practice. This method of meditation excites the nervous system, activating parts of the brain responsible for motion. This method should be practiced with specific goals in mind, but shouldn't be used in place of presence meditation. I'll be explaining more about visualization in the chapter Creative Visualization.

The next two methods are technology based styles and require less discipline and technique. This doesn't mean you should skip the above and just do these; it simply means they are a great complement as we practice to improve our technical abilities. Each style has its place.

Audio enhancement meditation requires the use of sounds such as chanting, gonging, singing bells, and my personal favorite, binaural beats.

Binaural beats are the product of a theory called brainwave entrainment that aims at achieving hemisphere synchronization, or a state where the brainwave pattern of left and right hemispheres of the brain become alike. Some researchers believe that humans have practiced similar methods of brainwave entrainment for thousands of years with use of various tools such as drums, flickering sunlight, singing bowls, gonging, and chanting.

Binaural beats are two tones that are slightly different than each other that produce a "beat" that sort of sounds like *wah wah wah* when listened to. It's best to listen to binaural beats with stereo headphones because of how they're designed. The sound you hear is two tones that are similar in frequency playing at the same time, producing a specific, subsonic beat. For example, if you played a 495Hz tone and 505Hz tone, the result would be a subsonic 10Hz beat. The listener will experience a stimulation of the brain waves, resulting in specific frequencies that range from Alpha, Beta, Delta, Theta, and Gamma. Each frequency stimulates different states including creativity, relaxation, alertness, and more.

The final method of meditation is guided. Guided meditations can be practiced with recordings or by attending a guided meditation class. Typically, these meditations are structured very similar to a style of hypnosis. The idea is that the instructor will use various awareness techniques to help the student become very relaxed and access their subconscious mind. From there, the instructor may implant specific suggestions or entice the student to bring up past memories or even past lives. Guided meditations can be very effective in counseling a subject into changing specific behaviours and can have great benefits. Some guided meditation recordings will also have binaural beats in the background to assist in the induction. There will be various guided meditations available on this book's website that pertain to specific chapters to help with dream manifestation.

I've found some evidence that the best way to implement these methods into daily life for optimal results is to practice intention meditation first thing in the morning, visualization meditation in the middle of the day, then binaural beats and/or guided meditation in the evening. This sets your mind into a positive, relaxed state while slowly building into a creative, productive motion.

There are some other methods of meditation that are far above and beyond those that can be done at home. I've read of but have not yet experienced some methods that use electromagnets near the frontal lobe to actually stimulate parts of the brain that can induce incredible sensations, including intense intuitive and out-of-body experiences. These are done in the safety of a laboratory and should not be attempted without educated supervision.

Sensory Deprivation

Intention meditation works on a concept I've come across known as *sensory deprivation.* Studies have shown that through depriving our senses of external stimulus, we can influence them to become hyper aware. When we meditate, we are aware of our surroundings, though we're not specifically focusing on any particular stimulus. Our eyes are usually closed, we're sitting still, and we're usually in a quiet area. For the most part, our senses are being deprived of any significant stimulus, and as a product of this, our senses become heightened temporarily, looking for some sort of experience to stimulate them. As a result, our senses can remain stimulated for up to forty-eight hours. It's my belief that as our five physical senses increase, our *sixth sense*, or intuition, also increases (we'll talk about this a bit more in the element Intuitive Feedback).

There is an interesting meditation tool created by Dr. John C Tilly in 1954 called an Isolation Tank or Sensory Deprivation Tank. These tanks are becoming very popular all over the world, and with good reason. Basically, this tank is big enough for one or two people to lie in comfortably and is filled with water and about one thousand pounds of Epsom salts. The air and water inside the tank are kept at body temperature, and the Epsom salts make your body completely buoyant. The tank is closed and keeps all of the sound and light out, so as the name implies, all of your senses are deprived. You lie in tank for between sixty to ninety minutes, and experiences have been described as peace, tranquility, and almost instant meditation. Some people have claimed to have an immediate out-of-body, natural, psychedelic-like experience.

This intense deprivation of the senses causes your brain to become hyperaware, making all of your senses increase. Though the sensory deprivation tank is an accelerated method of increasing our senses, regular meditation has been shown to do this, as well. As mentioned earlier, through depriving our physical senses during meditation, we increase their sensitivity while also increasing the effectiveness of our sixth sense. This hyperawareness has been shown to last for up to forty-eight hours, which is why I suggest meditation being a daily practice.

This is not just hokey pokey, superstitious belief. In The Shift, I talk about thoughts and ESP and how this type of information is far from just "witchcraft" like it's been touted as in the past. Meditation has been stated as a necessary component to increasing the ability to access hidden parts of our mind and consciousness. Again, if you have an interest in learning how meditation can increase your psychic intuition and awareness, look up some books by Harold Sherman; he's definitely one of the best sources I've found to date.

How To Meditate (In Three Steps)

Although there are many different methods of meditation there is one simple way I like to teach my students. If you follow these three steps and have patience with yourself you will succeed; it's guaranteed.

1) Find a comfortable place in any posture you choose and take five deep breaths, in your nose and out your mouth. Increasing the oxygen in your body will help you focus and remain relaxed. After this you can breathe naturally in and out your mouth.

2) Start by placing your awareness on every part of your body starting with your toes. Feel your toes and take two full breaths, in and out. Then move your awareness to your ankles and take two full breaths. Repeat this all the way up your body, relaxing every muscle.

3) When you've finished relaxing every muscle in your body start counting backwards from 99 with every

inhale. *<Inhale>"99..."* *<exhale>*. *<Inhale>* *"98..."* *<exhale>* and so on. If you notice your thoughts start to fade you can let go of the counting and come back to your breath. If the thoughts start to overwhelm you again you can begin counting again.

That's it! Meditation can be challenging, most times only because of the misconceptions we have of it. By simply sticking to these three steps, everyday no matter what you will start to notice the benefits of meditation in no time.

28 Days of Meditation

Throughout teaching meditation and taking my own journey, I've faced some challenges that have lead me to create this meditation website and course. Though you can go to the website and subscribe to learn you can also do so simply from the directions here. The idea is pretty simple. Basically, you meditate for twenty-eight days and journal the experience every day. Journaling your meditation keeps you accountable and makes it much harder to skip a day. You start Day One with just one minute of meditation, that's it. Sit in a comfortable position, set your timer for one minute, meditate (following the three steps), then journal the experience. It's really that simple.

You add one minute every day until you eventually get to twenty-eight days and twenty-eight minutes. So Day Two will be two minutes, Day Three will be three minutes, etc. You're welcome to meditate for more than your required minutes but the idea is that you're only responsible for the number you're on. After the twenty-eight days, you can revert back to twenty minutes per day if you'd like. The course is most effective if you finish right to the twenty-eight day mark. By that time, you will have created a routine and have kept yourself accountable by journaling every day. After the twenty-eight day mark, you can also give up the journaling, but some people enjoy it.

If you think twenty-eight days is too long to commit to, then try fourteen, but whatever you do, set a goal and *stick to it*. It's easy to make excuses and say that you don't have time, but there's an old Zen proverb that says it best. "Everyone should meditate for at least twenty minutes per day unless they're too busy; then they should meditate for an hour." Make time, you'll be glad you did.

Other Mindfulness Practices

Although I believe that meditation is the most effective method of practicing mindfulness, there are others that can be a very enjoyable and affective addition to your practice. A very common and affective form of mindfulness practice is yoga. Yoga allows the subject to push their body to find their edge while being present in the moment, away from emotions that have no place in the practice. By focusing on the breath and the body, the practitioner is far away from the stresses of the day. There are various styles of yoga including Hatha, Bikram, Ashtanga, Anusara, Moksha, Vinyasa, and others. Yoga is something I try to practice at least once a week, which I have found is a great addition to my mindfulness practice and physical activity.

Another method of mindfulness I enjoy very much is dance.

Dance is very similar to yoga in that it helps us focus on our body's movement and rhythm, distracting us from our stresses and worries. There are countless styles of dance, and all are a fantastic way to get your body moving and become present in the moment.

Finally, the method of mindfulness that has its roots deep in my life is martial arts training. Nearly all traditional martial arts practice mindfulness and presence in one form or another. Whether it's during kata practice, contact sparring, or actual meditation, martial arts can be an excellent form of mindfulness, bringing peace and tranquility to the student's experience.

Mindfulness is something that can be added to virtually any daily practice. Cooking, cleaning, running, walking, and even driving can all be exercises in mindfulness. When you find yourself drifting off, thinking about your past or future, try bringing yourself back to your breath and anchor yourself in the present moment. Remember that time is an illusion, and the only moment that ever exists is right now.

----------WARNING----------

The following two chapters are very controversial. They will be offering ideas, theories, and concepts that may be unacceptable to some and exceptionally confusing to others. If you dislike complex scientific theories and would like to keep it simple, you do not need to read these chapters to find value in this book. I've simply included them to offer some food for thought for those who like to think outside the box. At this point, you have two choices:

End your studies here and use what you've learned to manifest the life of your dreams,

Or

Keep an open mind, continue down the rabbit hole, and find your own truth.

I've put a lot of work into researching this information and have pondered these ideas for quite some time. I by no means claim to be a scientist, expert, or authority on these concepts, but rather an eager student of possibility and, admittedly, a slave to curiosity. If you are choosing to read on, feel free to stop at any time and close the book. However, if you choose to continue and feel the desire to do some of your own research, I strongly suggest you do; the answers are there for those who wish to find them.

Again, you **do not** need to read these chapters to benefit from the concepts in this book, so please do not feel obligated.

THE UNDERWORLD

QUANTUM THEORY

For many people, this chapter may cause some serious dissonance. Attributing quantum theory to anything to do with spirituality, the law of attraction, metaphysics, manifesting dreams, or any of it usually causes quite a stir. People don't like it—in fact many hate it—but I'm ok with that. Others may struggle to get through it, suffering a seemingly endless boredom or confusion, and for that, I apologize, but give it a chance; something may pop out and inspire you.

This chapter is not intended to prove to anyone that the information that comes after it is true because that may never be possible in conventional means. I'm including this chapter to invite you to start digging for yourself and consider that perhaps everything we thought we knew is in fact much stranger than fiction. Maybe reality isn't as it seems, and maybe there is much more to it than we ever imagined.

I'm not a scientist or a formal researcher, so I've decided to hand this chapter over to someone more qualified to write it because, as I mentioned, this might be an area where some disagreements arise. I'm going to concede that I don't fully understand any of the experiments we're going to share, as most people, including those who proposed them in the first place, don't. Quantum theory is science, not philosophy, so I know it's important for me to be very careful how I allow the ideas to be presented and to not suggest things that may appear as "hopeful thinking".

In saying all of this, I wouldn't waste my time putting it in the book if I didn't think it was important. To me, this chapter serves as a means of stirring up questions like "What if?" and "Is it possible?" because if any of these things are possible, which many scientists have—and still are—dedicating their lives to, then we have a lot to learn about what we think is real.

Let's talk about what "real" really is for a moment. For those of you who have seen the movie *The Matrix* this concept might be familiar. "Real" might be understood as anything we can measure with our five senses, each of which are experienced through chemical reactions in our brains. What is "real" then can only be defined as something we experience subjectively through a physical means. Reality then seems to be dependent upon physics in order to exist.

This is where I'm going to hand the chapter over to friend and colleague, Ghislain d'Entremont. Ghislain is a neuroscientific research student and truly super smart guy. You can find some of his wellness related research in the "Research" section at www.elevatedwellness.org.The next bit of information is going to be out of this world, so I hope you enjoy it. I'll see you on the other side.

Enter: Ghislain d'Entremont, Science Whiz

In this chapter, I will present some of the central concepts and ideas of quantum physics. We will not get into the mathematical details of quantum mechanics, but it's important to understand that many of these concepts are actually completely derived from mathematics. For example, when I start talking about parallel universes, don't assume that we've actually seen parallel universes with our bare eyes or by staring through a microscope.

Parallel universes are ideas created in minds of scientists that help explain the mathematics of quantum mechanics and vice-versa. In the cases where experiments actually have been done to support a theory or hypothesis, I will do my best to describe the experiment in such a way as to get the point across while still maintaining the important details of the experiment. Keep an open mind and try your best to conceptualize these madly abstract ideas and to understand their implications. The purpose of this chapter is to make you marvel at how little we truly know about our reality and existence.

Copenhagen Interpretation

First, let's establish why there is 'quantum' in 'quantum physics'. The premise is simple; light is not a stream of energy but rather a sequence of particles, photons. Imagine shooting a BB gun frequently enough that the individual BBs become indistinguishable and start looking like one beam of BBs. I am describing to you light as being made up of individual bits, as being quantized, hence, quantum physics. Quantum physics is the field of study, whereas quantum mechanics are the rules, the laws that particles follow.

The Copenhagen Interpretation was simply the first attempt of physicists to explain the natural world at the sub-atomic level with respect to quantum mechanics. Conceptually, many of the principles of the Copenhagen Interpretation are still widely accepted. The interpretation is fascinating because it is incredibly counterintuitive. As humans, we perceive only a miniscule portion of reality. We do not see, hear, or smell atoms, electromagnetism, gravity, energy, etc. Our senses do not allow it. Therefore, our perception of reality is limited.

Classical physics describes the physics of objects and space at the level at which we, humans, operate—on the scale of footballs, turkey sandwiches, dogs and trees. Classical physics is, therefore, intuitive. Here's a formal and brief summary: physical objects exist at definite places in space and time. They exist at a definite place at a definite time. This is intuitive. If you throw a baseball to a friend wearing a baseball glove, the ball finds itself either in OR out of the glove—never both in AND out of the glove. Well, quantum mechanics suggests otherwise. It suggests that at a sub-atomic level, the ball really can be both in AND out of the glove at the same time.

Imagine any one element you learned about in ninth grade chemistry. All right, now let's take a particle from that element—let's say an electron. If you picture an electron, you probably picture some sort of a floating sphere, a ball of sorts. Well, the culmination of physics results in the early 20th century left numerous physicists thinking that an electron is more than just a ball of matter. Instead, it suggested that an electron is more like a wave.

That's right. Think of waves by the beach. An electron or any other kind of particle is a wave that is at many places all at once. Once you try to measure—to calculate the speed or the position—of this wave, however, the wave collapses into a particle. When I say that the wave collapses, I mean that it stops behaving like a wave and starts behaving like a particle, like a ball of matter—the way you are used to thinking about it.

The dichotomous description of the matter—as a wave and a particle—is known as the wave-particle duality or the complementarity principle, and it is the central aspect of the Copenhagen Interpretation. In the section on Young's Double Split Experiment, we will look at one of the primary physics experiments that laid the groundwork for the Copenhagen Interpretation.

When a particle is behaving like a wave, you can think of it as being in multiple places at once. The exact position of the particle, if measured, will be at any one of its possible places with a given probability. These probabilities are determined by a wave function—a mathematical description of the particle/wave. This phenomenon of matter being at multiple places/states all at the same time is called superposition. We will see in the section on Schrodinger's Cat the strange consequences of superposition.

Schrodinger's Cat

Recall that matter can behave like a particle some of time and a wave the rest of the time (wave/particle duality). Also, remember that matter behaves like a wave until it is *observed,* at which points it starts behaving like a particle. For now, let's assume that this observer is a conscious being. That is, until a conscious being in some way observes a wave/particle, it behaves like a wave, and once observed, it behaves like a particle. Ok, keep that assumption in mind. I'm going to introduce a thought experiment proposed by Schrodinger (mathematician) that takes the basic principles of quantum mechanics we've been discussing at the sub-atomic level and applies it to the scale of cats and boxes to give you Schrodinger's Cat.

Note: No cats were harmed in the pondering of Schrodinger's Cat

In this thought experiment, a cat is trapped in a steel chamber with a Geiger counter with which it cannot interfere. (A Geiger counter is an instrument that measures radiation). The Geiger counter contains just enough radioactive substance so that over the course of an hour, one atom decays and does not decay with equal probability (i.e. there is a 50 percent chance that the atom decays and a 50 percent chance that it does not). The chamber setup is such that if an atom does decay, a small flask of hydrocyanic acid will shatter inside the steel chamber, killing the cat.

Applying some of the principles of quantum mechanics

according to some variation of the Copenhagen Interpretation, after precisely one hour, the cat would be both dead and alive simultaneously (superposition). Only when a conscious observer opens the steel chamber to observe (measure) in what state the cat remains would the wave function describing the dual states of the cat's mortality assume one of the two states, rendering the cat either dead or alive.

But how could a cat be both dead and alive? It's intuitive nonsense. Also, how could a human observation determine its fate? It just seems like some spooky science fiction.

Neils Bohr (scientist) didn't perceive the experiment as being problematic because of his alternative take on the Copenhagen Interpretation. He believed the cat would be either dead or alive before the intervention of a conscious observer because even the unconscious detection of the atom decaying would result in the wave function collapsing. Specifically, the implication was that the wave function describing the atom would collapse prior to a human opening the chamber because of the *observation* (measurement) made by the Geiger counter. In this case, the cat would in fact be dead or alive after an hour, not both.

The results from a 2006 study by Carpenter and Anderson entitled *The death of Schrodinger's cat and the consciousness-based collapse of the quantum wave-function collapse* suggest that any measurement conscious or unconscious is sufficient to elicit a wave function collapse, naturally supporting Bohr's view.

's Double Slit Experiment

Young's Double Split Experiment is one of earliest (1801) physics experiments demonstrating wave-particle duality in photons and matter. Try your best to clear your mind of what you've already read about matter behaving at times like a particle and at times like a wave. Imagine that you perceived the microscopic physical world in terms of simple particles, atoms and molecules—the way you likely did for the majority of your life—then try to fathom the results of the experiment described below.

Thomas Young set up the experiment to lend support to the unpopular hypothesis at the time that light behaved like a wave. The experiment was simple: direct light toward a barrier with two slits and record the light that goes through on the other side of the barrier. The light that is recorded on the other side of the barrier is represented by light patches on a dark surface—let's call this surface (recording instrument) a backboard from this point on. Now, thinking of light as being a beam of particles—photons in this instance—you would expect there to be two light strips on the backboard, one for each slit. In other words, you would expect the barrier to create a shadow on the backboard for where the slits are located. The results, however, were quite different. The backboard, after beaming light at the barrier, had a sequence of light and dark patches. The backboard had more than two light strips. Thinking of light as particle, this makes no sense. However, thinking of light as a wave, the results are a perfect fit!

All right, so let's think about waves to reason this out. When two waves run into each other, interfere with each other, they create what is known as an interference pattern. The latter is characterized by constructive and destructive interferences. Using water waves as an example, constructive interference happens when the peaks of two different waves interfere, becoming one peak, doubling in height. Destructive interference happens when the peak of one wave and the trough of another interfere, becoming one flat wave, therefore cancelling each other out. This makes sense. In the case of light waves, a peak would be described by a greater light intensity and a trough by lower (or non-existent) light intensity.

Now let's describe what we would expect the light to do if it behaved as a wave. When the light wave would reach the barrier with two slits, it would create two separate waves coming out of the other side of the barrier, one for each split. These two waves would then interfere with each other as they made their way to the backboard, forming an interference pattern on the backboard. This means that we would see a sequence of light and dark patches on the backboard—exactly the results of Young's experiment! These findings supported the idea that light behaves as both a wave and a particle.

With this said, Young did not predict that actual matter would exhibit a similar wave-particle duality. In later years, however, the experiment was done with an electron beam—an apparatus which shoots out electrons. The results were similar. An interference pattern appeared on the backboard, implying that matter also has this wave-particle duality, at least at smaller scales.

Quantum Entanglement

So far, we've seen some bizarre consequences of quantum mechanics, but we've just gotten started. The more we dig deep, the weirder the implications of these physical laws become. Next up is quantum entanglement, a phenomenon which essentially resembles particle telepathy.

Quantum entanglement is one of the central concepts of quantum mechanics. Two or more particles can be grouped in such a way that their associated states are not independent of each other. This is to say that two particles which exist in two separate and distant locations can somehow affect each other's behavior. Such particles are said to be entangled. The idea is that measuring the state of an entangled particle will collapse its wave function to a definite state, which would then immediately collapse the wave function of the other entangled particle to a definite state, regardless of the distance between these two particles. If this sounds like telepathy to you, then you understand the concept.

What makes this concept even more interesting is that it's been tested experimentally. One method for creating two entangled particles is to start with a single particle and allow it to decay into two lower energy particles. A team of Japanese scientists did this by splitting single photons into two lower energy photons. The photons travelled through separate optical fibers, each of around one hundred fifty kilometers of length. The photons that made it all the way to the end of the wires were measured and verified to be entangled with their counterparts three hundred kilometres away.

Parallel Universes/ Multiverses

A multiverse is essentially a meta-universe, or a collection of universes. Mark Tegmark, a professor of cosmology of astronomy, posits that there are four multiverse levels defined descriptively as follows:

1. Beyond our cosmic horizon

2. Other post-inflation bubbles

3. Quantum many-worlds

4. Other mathematical structures

I will focus on the first three because they are the less controversial and the most interesting.

<u>Level I Multiverse</u>

The furthest we can observe outward from our universe is 4 * 10^26 meters (42 billion light-years). A light-year is simply the distance that light travels in a vacuum (empty space) in one year. This range defines the diameter of a parallel universe. Think of these parallel universes as being inflated balls of matter and space forty-two billion light-years across. These parallel universes differ only in their initial arrangements of matter, their fundamental laws of nature, and their constants are identical. This means that gravity and the rest of it remains the same in these parallel universes, but the ways particles were set up at the beginning of these universes are different. Furthermore, since space is infinite, there exist infinitely many parallel universes.

Taken together, this implies that there must be parallel universes identical to our own. By utilizing basic statistics, we can calculate the average distance of the nearest duplicate of our universe to ourselves. The estimate distance between our universes and our duplicate universe is ten to the power of ten to the power of one hundred eighteen meters, which is an incomprehensibly large distance. But this distance is beside the point. The point is that *there is* an identical universe to our own out there. And since this universe is identical in every way, there must exist your doppelganger in that universe, somewhere out there. Yes, a certain interpretation of quantum mechanics suggests that there really is another you.

Level II Multiverse

A Level I multiverse exists within a bubble. And there exists many of these bubbles, and thus parallel Level I multiverses. Notice that the terms are important to not get mixed up. So let's summarize. We live in a universe, and there exists many other universes around ours called parallel universes. Now imagine taking all these parallel universes and putting them into a transparent bag or a bubble. We are then left with a level I multiverse. Still with me? Now imagine that we have many of these bubbles, many of these level I multiverses. So we have parallel level I multiverses. Finally, if we take all these parallel level I multiverses and put them into an even bigger bubble, we get our level II multiverse. It's kind of like playing with Russian dolls.

All the parallel level I multiverses in the level II multiverse differ in their physical constants, particle types, and dimensionalities. This means that gravity and other fundamental laws of nature are actually different from one level I multiverse to the next.

Level III Multiverse

In the level I multiverse, there exist parallel universes elsewhere in space. However, in the level III multiverse, parallel universes exist 'elsewhere', but with 'elsewhere' defined as an abstract realm of all possible states. If this makes sense to you, you *don't* understand the concept. What I am saying is that this is an extremely abstract reality that we conjure based on pure mathematics so we (as humans) are not meant to be able to understand these concepts intuitively. But we can try the best we can, and be awe inspired by the wonder of this possible reality that tests the limits of our imaginations.

In any case, this idea of the level III multiverse is derived from the many worlds interpretation of quantum mechanics, presented in 1957 by Hugh Everett III. Everett postulated that instead of a wave function collapsing to one definite state, it perseveres as a wave assuming multiple states simultaneously, all possible definitive states exist superimposed on each other.

Notice that this differs slightly from the Copenhagen Interpretation we presented earlier in the chapter. This different interpretation implies that in the level III multiverse, all possible outcomes (all states that a wave function could collapse to) of an event exist as parallel universes. In other words, there exist many worlds, one for every outcome of a given event. This is crazy. I am telling you that every possible thing that ever could have happened has actually happened, but just in different universes. Extending this a little further, this means that some of the things you regretted not doing in your life were actually done by you, just in different universes.

---Exit Ghislian---

For references on this chapter, visit the end of the book.

I hope you found Ghislian's research interesting, I know I did. The big thing about asking these questions is that the treasure isn't in the answers; it's in the bigger questions. When we know that anything is possible, we become free to dream, to imagine anything we desire. When something isn't impossible, it becomes ours.

THE SHIFT

QUANTUM FOOLERY

I'm going to warn you; the next few pages get a little weird. The ideas I'm sharing here are not going to be taken lightly by some people, and others may think I'm completely whacked...but I'm cool with it. As always, take what I say here and see how it resonates with you personally.

If we understand that there could be multiple realities and universes, all existing at the same time, and that there could be an infinite amount of those realities and universes, then it has to be possible that the reality we're looking to experience exists out there, as well. There has to be a reality where you have the dream job, dream car, or dream partner. There's a reality where you wake up excited almost every day, and smiling is a common occurrence. But how would we get to that reality? How can we go from here to there? That's where quantum shifting comes in to play.

Quantum shifting is a concept that suggests we can actually shift from one reality or universe to another by *emotionally* aligning ourselves with that reality. With quantum shifting, we can shift to other realities that are already happening right now. I know, it sounds crazy.

I warned you! This is going to require creativity, so stay with me here. You don't have to understand or even believe in quantum shifting for the rest of this book to work, so if at any point in time you find yourself struggling to follow along, feel free to end the journey here.

Let's slow down for a minute. There's another concept we should explore first. I initially came across this idea from author Steve Pavlina, and it completely blew my mind. The concept battles with the ideas of objective reality and subjective reality. Objective reality is the idea that we are all just experiencing different observational points of the same reality, or what I'm seeing is just a viewpoint of the same reality you're seeing. In objective reality, we're all just observing the same plain of existence from different centers. In this world, you are a character in a dream, and that dream is the real, physical world.

Subjective reality is a little different, and you're going to have to use your imagination with this one. The basis of subjective reality is that the reality you're experiencing is completely yours and yours alone. Everyone inside your reality is actually a projection of the beliefs and ideas you hold about that person. In a subjective reality, other people, places, and things may be influenced by co-creation, but in your perspective, they are dominantly the version you're creating them to be. In this reality, you are not only the character in the dream, but you are also the dreamer. You are both the character and the world around it, existing at the same time. Sleeping dreams are like little subjective realities being experienced. In dreams, we are both the dreamer and the character experiencing the dream.

This concept can cause a little bit of dissonance in some people because accepting it means you may also have to accept that anything you've experienced in your life, good or bad, may have been—for the most part—a creation of your own. For a lot of people, this might be where the book gets closed, but I invite you to let go of any resistant feelings you're experiencing and continue reading on; there's a method to this madness.

So if subjective reality were a real thing, then that would mean that the pages you're reading right now are actually an aspect of your own consciousness communicating with you. In fact, everything you've ever read, seen, heard, or experienced in your entire life would have been a projection of your own consciousness. Kind of mind blowing, huh?

You might be wondering how the idea of subjective reality ties in with quantum shifting to parallel universes? This is another aspect that requires some imagination. For the theory of quantum shifting to work, we would have to shift our entire reality, or universe, as our perspective shifted. That means that if you wanted to shift to the reality where you have the dream job, you'd also have to shift to a reality where the boss that's going to hire you also wanted you to have that dream job. Everything would have to come with you as you shifted. Sound a little nutty? Hear me out.

If there are multiple, seemingly parallel universes and realities, and we're all just experiencing one of those realities subjectively, then perhaps we're able to incrementally shift our awareness or observational point to one of these parallel universes. Maybe we're able to "tune in" to one of these other probable realities. These shifts might be so minute and small that we wouldn't even notice them most of the time.

Remember how we learned that particles hold a super position before they're observed? What if these quantum shifts happened at such an incredibly microscopic or *quantum* level that they smoothly transitioned without us even realizing it? This may sound a bit like the twilight zone, but it's exactly what many authors, researchers, physicists, and more have been suggesting for hundreds, maybe even thousands of years.

Ok, but if this theory is correct, and we could shift through parallel realities and universes, and our own consciousness is projecting back to itself, then wouldn't we experience some sort of conscious evidence? Well, maybe we do.

Have you ever had a gut feeling or intuition about something that came true? Have you ever thought of someone and had them call at the same time? These events are commonly regarded as coincidence to the skeptic, but to many, these events are called "synchronicities" and are believed to be a clear indication of our reflected internal consciousness. Seeing minor changes in our reality may point to the process of a much larger manifestation on the way. Maybe you keep seeing that dream car or you run into someone who you've been meaning to get in touch with. Whatever they may be these events happen all around us. Deja Vu is also believed to be a similar type of phenomena, but there's a lot less literary evidence out there for me to want to really get into that.

After diving into this stuff deep enough, the question of whether or not this was possible started to fade for me, and I moved more toward the question of what it means for me personally and for those around me. If the reality we experience really is ours and ours alone, and the people, places, and things we experience are part of our own conscious creation, then what can that mean for the world? Couldn't we all start to shift the world around us by shifting our own beliefs and fears? How can we use this to improve our lives and the lives of those around us? These questions, paired with a couple of years of research, are what inspired me to write this book.

Again, we may be wondering how something so substantial could go hidden throughout the entire human experience; but maybe it didn't. We've already explored that the act of observing a particle may affect its position as a wave or particle, and mystics, spiritualists, philosophers, and many others have suggested that our beliefs, thoughts, and actions toward others and ourselves could also influence the reality around us. Henry Ford said, "Whether you think you can or can't, you're right." Napoleon Hill wrote, "*Whatever the* mind can conceive and believe, it can achieve." Thomas Edison, Nikola Tesla, Gregg Braden, Masaru Emoto, and many others have pondered these possibilities.

The Law Of Attraction

Ester Hicks, in her book, *The Law of Attraction*, writes, "Is it possible to be the visionary and the actionary of your own life? Not only possible, it's the way most of you intended it to be. It's the best of all worlds."

For those who have never heard of the law of attraction, let me give you a little rundown. The law of attraction (or LOA) is the idea that our thoughts and emotions physically attract things to us from our external world. According to LOA, through utilizing our emotions, thoughts, actions, and even language, we can begin to *attract* experiences into our lives. By virtue of this idea, if we wanted to attract a dream car or dream house, we can use the power of thoughts and emotions to do so. There have been many books and videos created on the subject, including Rhonda Byrne's movie and book titled *The Secret* as well as many of her others, such as *The Hero*, *The Power*, and more. Esther Hicks, the author mentioned above, as well as many others, such as Bob Proctor, Jack Canfield, and more, have also spoken and written about the law of attraction.

The general concept and understanding of the law of attraction is that "if you think positive thoughts, you will attract positive things". This sounds pretty simple, and according to countless supporters, followers, and advocates, it is. "Just think positive!" That's it. But is it? The research I've found suggests there's much more to actualizing your dreams than simply thinking positive, and that's what this book is all about. Thoughts are a very important aspect, but there's a lot more to it, and we're going to explore some of these ideas and concepts in the chapters to come.

The law of attraction *was* my first taste of learning how to manifest our realities and create our dreams, but it didn't satisfy my continued craving for understanding. I like to think of the law of attraction as the "gateway drug" of universal concepts and metaphysics—a nice, but incomplete introduction. It often focuses a lot on material things rather than really digging to the core of what we all desire: happiness and passion. According to the law of attraction, if you and I had the same level of desire for an identical thing or person and "thought positively", despite our efforts, one of us would have to go without. One of us would have to accept that they aren't getting the thing they desired. Perhaps fate steered their desire elsewhere? Maybe they realized they didn't desire the thing as much as they wanted? Maybe, or maybe there's a missing piece.

From the perspective of quantum shifting, the law of attraction is actually a physical representation of a non-physical event. Manifestation is a much more complex process. We experience reality in the third dimension, but there are in fact many other higher dimensions we don't perceive. When we experience a particular desired situation *attracting* to us in our third dimensional reality, it is also changing and shifting on the higher dimensions, which are beyond our perception. On those dimensions, reality is actually forming out of pure potential, morphing into potential realities, and the reality *we* experience is determined by the alignment of our own subjective experience. We might feel like these desires are being *attracted* to us (such as the dream car or dream job), but in fact, we're moving or shifting our *observational experience* into alignment with that reality—a reality which has been manifested from pure potential.

These realities are created as potential outcomes generated by our individual thoughts, choices, actions, and expectations. An example would be the possible realities you could experience if you choose to go to work or not. If you choose to go to work, you open one set of potential future probabilities, and if you choose not to go, you open up a different set of probabilities. Our desires work the same way, and whether or not we manifest them into our experience is also determined by these thoughts, choices, actions, and expectations. When we use the term "attract", we're implying the desirable or undesirable situation was outside of us, whereas I'm proposing that our manifestations come from within.

To put it simply, the realities each of us experience are unique to us, the individual. What you perceive is not what I perceive, and what I perceive is not what you perceive. You are both the character in the dream *and* the dreamer. According to this theory, if we both desired the same thing, we could potentially *both* get it in our own individual realities with each of us experiencing a separate outcome—an outcome that again is determined by our thoughts, choices, actions, and expectations.

Some people may experience difficulty in accepting that they've manifested a world with so much pain and suffering, but if this theory is correct, then we've simply *shifted* to a reality where these things are happening. It doesn't mean we've intentionally or unintentionally manifested it. However, it does mean we can change it.

So if this is all true, then we could tap into an unlimited

abundance that would always be present, limited only by our minds. Besides exploring aspects of how to make this possible, this book also helps you dig deep into your heart and mind to find out what it is you *really* desire and how to actually manifest that easily and effortlessly into your life. Toys are nice, but they don't last forever. What I'm offering in this book is a strategic guide to a life of happiness, love, and excitement. After all, it's not the things that make us happy; it's the happy that makes us happy. The best part is, when you're happy, you'll get to have lots of great things, too, you'll get the full HD experience.

There are other concepts that share these ideas, including Deepak Chopra's *The Seven Spiritual Laws of Success,* David Deangelo's *The 77 Laws of Success and Dating*, and Bob Proctor's *The 11 Forgotten Laws*, among many more. If I didn't know better, I'd have to say we're on to something here...

Look, I know this is deep, and I know you're thinking, "huh?" but have an open mind and try to stay with me.

One very valuable thing that the law of attraction offers is the idea of being mindful of our thoughts. Let's ponder thoughts for a moment. What are they? Where do they come from? What do they mean? How do they affect the world around us? Scientists have been able to measure thoughts for many years now. In fact, an effort called the Global Consciousness Project, or GCP, is dedicated to just that. The GCP is a parapsychology experiment that started in 1998 to try to detect a global consciousness with the use of a device called a random event generator. Basically, these generators act like a coin flipping machine, creating completely random numbers. Massive global events such as the Twin Tower disaster in 2001 have shown to affect the results to a clear, measurable degree. There have been multiple measurements taken during major global events, and they've been compiling data from projects as far back as the 1970s. The basic idea they suggest is that thoughts can travel worldwide as fast, if not faster, than the speed of light. That means that according to the GCP, your thoughts are part of a worldwide consciousness grid that interacts with the rest of the geographical world as quickly as you think them.

According to researchers, thoughts are found to have varying electromagnetic properties. Light is also electromagnetic, and it travels fast. There are spectrums of light that are far beyond our visual limitations, which are measured by special devices. So, hypothetically speaking, if thoughts are made out of the same type of substance as light, and light can travel across the world and be interpreted by a receiver on the other end, couldn't thoughts do the same thing? What if our brains had the ability to receive thoughts outside of our own?

Why Did I Attract That?

A common woe for believers of the law of attraction is the experience of contrast. According to the law of attraction, if an unwanted situation manifests, then the person experiencing it must have attracted it to themselves through their thoughts. The issue is, seemingly bad situations might actually be leading you to the thing you want, but because you become so distraught over the thing you didn't want, you shift even further away from the thing you do. In other words, if you trust that your discomfort from a contrasting situation is leading you to what you desire, then you will allow it to come to you even quicker. You didn't attract contrast; you manifested it because it's leading to your highest potential.

Extra Sensory Perception

We talked about Extra Sensory Perception in Intuitive Feedback, and I wanted to touch on it again. Extra Sensory Perception, or ESP, is defined as perception or communication outside of what is considered "normal" in modern day science. This means outside of the ability to measure it with our five senses. Author Harold Sherman (1898 – 1987) wrote over twenty books on various aspects of ESP and conducted hundreds of experiments in his lifetime. He was renowned in the field of psychic research and claimed to have received psychic communication with famous Arctic explorer, Sir Hubert Wilkins, on many occasions. He also helped the police solve multiple cases, including missing persons and more. Sherman and many others have offered a very scientific approach to an often believed to be pseudoscience phenomena.

Remember those peculiar coincidences we talked about earlier called synchronicities? Well, synchronicities are believed to be evidence that your internal consciousness is interacting with the world around you. Believers see them as little hints that your thoughts are actually creating the reality you perceive and experiencing "previews" of it on a small degree. Dr. Kirby Surprise holds a PhD in counseling psychology and wrote the book *Synchronicity: The Art of Coincidence, Choice and Unlocking the Mind.* He mentions in chapter six, Satori in a Can, "What you believe is a separate self, is a computational model of yourself placed on the stage with the rest of reality constructed around you. Remarkably, you have the ability to modify not only the reality that is on the stage, but you can change the representation of yourself, and your relationship to the reality you are constructing." In other words, your outside reality is a projection of your internal, psychological structure, and synchronicities are little mirror images of that internal world.

Act from the Heart

Our brains are electromagnetic emission instruments that send out information in the form of thoughts. As mentioned above, these thoughts can be picked up by other people as well as the world around us. As interesting as this is, more research has been showing that our hearts produce electromagnetic information five thousand times stronger than our brains. According to the Institute of Heartmath, our hearts produce an incredibly strong electromagnetic field that can be measured several feet away from the body. After knowing what we know about thoughts and how far they travel, it really makes this heart stuff interesting. This could mean that the emotions we *feel* send out much stronger signals than the thoughts we *think* do. Many spiritual beliefs also support the idea that our hearts are the true center of our intelligence.

This is also another concept that doesn't seem all that

unfamiliar, does it? How many times have we been told to "listen to your heart", "do what your heart tells you", or have felt *heartbroken*? It's widely believed and, no doubt, soon to be proven that there is a lot more to our emotions than we realize and that through understanding them, we can become capable of much more than we've ever imagined.

Consciousness

For those who are unfamiliar with consciousness, outside of the fact that you're awake and reading this right now, you might think of it as the *you* who is aware that there even is a you. It is the awareness *behind* your thoughts, behind your beliefs and patterns, at the subconscious level of your mind. I know this may sound confusing, so I'll ask you a few questions to maybe stimulate some ideas. When you think a thought, who is it that is thinking that thought? Is it *you*, the ego, the person? And is the thought you, and are you the thought, or is the thought a product of you? If the thought is a product of you, then where does it come from? On the other hand, if you are the thought, then who or what are you when there are no thoughts? Finally, are you the one thinking the thoughts, or are you the one observing the mind which is thinking the thoughts?

These are tough questions, and they might make your head hurt, but that's the idea. Remember, the true value isn't always in the answer but in the uncovering of even bigger questions.

Shifted Community?

So then, if quantum shifting is true, and we're shifting, moment by moment, to a different reality, a reality which is based on our expectation, then couldn't we ultimately shift to one where things were better? Where wars didn't exist and no one was hungry? Couldn't we begin to shift to this type of utopia by making sure we recycle, *resolving* drama and confrontation, giving to others, and being the change we want to see? If quantum shifting were true, then wouldn't it also be true that all we need to do to change the world is change ourselves—to live in alignment with such a world? Hmm.

Down, Down the Rabbit Hole

I know this stuff is deep, and don't worry, I don't expect you to understand this all yet (if ever). I'm introducing the *ideas* of quantum mechanics, quantum shifting, the law of attraction, and so on to propose that there is a lot more to reality than we understand. There is something to all of this, and people have known it for thousands of years. This book doesn't teach you all of the technical details because frankly, no one knows them yet. What this book teaches you is how to get the results you want *without* knowing the technical details. This book teaches you how to use what we *do* know to get the results you want without needing to know any of this scientific mumbo jumbo. So what I'm saying is that it's all just a little bit of nerdy science for those of you who are interested in reading it. For those of you who aren't, that's cool; this book is not about the how's, it's about the *what.*

AFTERTHOUGHT

In case you haven't realized it, there's a catch to practicing The Elements. The key to success is to follow your greatest excitement, chase your passion, and find your journey of happiness. That's when the rest of the fun stuff manifests itself along your path.

We talked about how we can remove some of the anxieties, limiting beliefs, and fears that may be holding us back in the first element, Emotional Self. These types of patterns are formed throughout our lives, and with personal development, patience, and self-forgiveness, we can learn to uproot them and free ourselves from their grips.

In the element, Physical Self, we learned that our bodies are temples and vehicles for our experience in life, and that by taking care of them, we can enhance the quality of our reality. Through being mindful of the foods we eat, exercising our bodies, and living a life of moderation, we can enjoy our experience while also ensuring a long and happy life.

The following elements start to introduce some of the various concepts, theories, and practices that have been used by many of the most successful people in the world for thousands of years. By building a strong foundation of mind and body with the first two elements, we open ourselves up to working in harmony with the universe and dancing with its energies in the following ones. We learn to observe the vibrations we're putting out into the world, to paint a vivid picture of the reality we wish to experience, and to align our lives into that desire so we can incrementally shift into its existence.

In the later elements, we begin to understand that our heart is a navigational system, and if we learn to listen to it, we can follow it to our greatest happiness. If we quiet our mind, step away from the distractions, and just listen...we might just hear the answers we've been looking for.

There's a time delay between our intention for a desire and its actual manifestation, and how we react in this period can have a tremendous effect on the duration of the delay itself. If we remain too attached to a desired outcome, in some cases, we may even prevent it from ever happening at all. We've learned that everything in natures has cycles: day turns to night, winter turns to summer, and after our peaks, we may experience a valley. If we remain confident and courageous in these times, however, we may just reach a higher peak than we could ever have imagined.

In The Now, we discussed the different types of meditation that can be used to help us manifest our dreams. I introduced some of the different technologies that are available, and also some of the meditation in motion practices like yoga, martial arts, and dance.

In the next chapter, The Underworld, we learned that there may be a lot more to reality than we perceive. When we get down to the very fundamental levels of matter, things start to act a lot differently and seem a little spooky. The book you're reading?

It's not a solid object. In fact, neither are your hands, your body, or anything else, for that matter. Most of what we are is actually empty space.

We learned that our observation has a real effect on reality as we perceive it, and that there may actually be an infinite amount of other realities where we exist just slightly different than we do here.

Finally, in The Shift, we pondered the theory of quantum shifting and the idea that perhaps the realities we're individually experiencing are actually unique to each of us, and the concepts of competition and lack are simply manifestations of our own expectations. We learned that our thoughts can be measured and have an impact on the world around us. We also discussed the practice of extra sensory perception and some of the cool experiments that have been conducted in its context.

Though this book has a lot of concepts, ideas, and theories, it can really be summed up into the simple formula I shared in Intuitive Feedback: Passion + Action *despite* Fear = Limitless Potential. Every time I've fought, every time I've performed music, every time I've gotten on a stage to speak in front of people, and during so many of the other things I've been through, I've been afraid. Actually, I've been downright terrified. The thing is, I've learned to understand, accept, anticipate, and even *appreciate* the fear because it's one of the emotions that keep me remembering that *I care*. If we're not at least a little bit afraid, then it—whatever *it* is—obviously doesn't mean that much to us. We damn well better be afraid.

When we follow our greatest excitement and move forward *despite fear*, the universe conspires to mold into whatever it is we desire. Mountains move and miracles manifest. I promise you, if you apply this formula to your life, magical things will happen.

The world can distract us from our truth and pull us back into the holographic prison we create with our minds. Rather than being frustrated at where the world is today, we can be grateful that we're waking up in the middle of it, able to reap the benefits of technology while learning to manipulate reality to shape our dreams. We can use our gifts to make the world a better place in our own unique way by serving others through excitement and passion. There's never been a better time in history to be awake and alive.

This path of personal development and self-growth can seem intimidating, even a bit lonely. I assure you there are many, many others who share the same thirst for knowledge and hunger for a change. If you are a shy person, then I strongly urge you to do your best to work through those inhibitions and break out of your shell. Even if it means saying hello to one new person a day, it's a start.

Once we've figured out what it is that makes our hearts sing, we only need to learn to share it with our community. We will always manifest those who share our dream and see our vision as long as we open ourselves up to those around us. It's ok to be vulnerable. As Brené Brown once said, "Vulnerability sounds like truth and feels like courage."

I know you have what it takes. Dig deep, be honest, tell yourself you want it, and go for it. Find shelter from the fear and barrel through. The life of your dreams is closer than you've ever known.

Is It Really about "Thinking Positive?"

No, not really. It's important to understand where our thoughts come from and to allow them to provide us insight on our current alignment, but always being positive is a stretch. We simply need to remain *optimistic.* We have to understand and *know* that things are moving in the direction we want them to and challenge our doubts when they surface. Even the times that seem tough are ultimately leading to our greatest desire, the desire to be happy. Happy isn't a place we get to and settle in. It's a place that has its ups and downs but remains balanced when we work with it. Happiness is a journey, and when we learn to dance along the way, we really begin to see what it's all about.

Rather than worrying about whether our thoughts are *negative* or *positive,* which is really just an opinion, we simply need to direct them to be *productive* or *counterproductive.* Cultivating our mind, challenging our limiting beliefs, and remaining optimistic will ultimately cause our thoughts to be productive by default. Understanding that "negative" thoughts are simply our awareness alarming us that something is out of alignment can make even the most self-defeating thoughts become productive and, therefore, lead us back to alignment.

About Relationships

As I dove more into personal development and really heavily researched the habits of happy, successful people, I also started to realize some trends in the romantic relationships those people have. For many years, we've been led to believe that when two people come together, they become one. They take an oath, verbally or legally, to share each other's lives no matter what, through thick or thin, whatever may come. It seems fewer and fewer people are able to actually continue and maintain this responsibility, and the ones who are do it a completely different way.

The people who are able to stay together the longest and happiest are usually those who understand the true formula for a successful relationship. Instead of two people coming together as one, they realize that two people coming together should equal more than the sum of their parts. Rather than 1 + 1 = 1 they understand that the formula is actually 1 + 1 = 3.

The successful relationships in the world are often a partnership of two individual people following their greatest excitements and passions while *complementing* each other's. They don't hold each other back or limit their life experiences, but rather add to the richness of them. They practice courage and faith in one another while understanding that if you love something, you really do have to be willing to let it go. Through offering this freedom, we are rewarded with a life of love and happiness.

Each individual in these successful relationships is willing to have humility for themselves by facing their own shadows and working on things that they'd like to improve. They understand that while they are "good enough" as they are, it is also essential to be always willing to become an improved version of ourselves. As we grow physically, we must also grow emotionally, even when growth is painful.

Not all relationships are meant to be long-term. Some are meant to offer us lessons or contrast so we can be sure what we want, while others are meant to elevate us to a new level of potential. One thing we can be sure of is if we're willing to learn from each of them and let them go when the time has come, the quality of our relationships will continue to improve. As we evolve, our relationships evolve.

Did You Do Your Homework?

Be honest! It's easy to take shortcuts and procrastinate but what you put in you will get out. Remember, "Someday" is a disease that will take *your dreams* to the *grave* with you." Start the journey of living the life you want *right now*.

A Final Note

If you remember my introduction, you might recall that before I discovered The Elements, a lot had happened. My childhood was tough; I was getting over a messy relationship, and was learning some very valuable things about myself. What I didn't mention is what has happened since.

My relationship with my family continues to get better and more loving than I ever remember. My parents spend time with me together and actually respect and enjoy each other's company. They're both doing well and taking care of themselves; they make me proud more and more all of the time.

My relationships are richer and more loving than I ever remember and when they need to come to an end they part in love and ease.

I recently opened Elevated Wellness Center in Halifax, NS with my business partner Scott and we have an incredible team working with us. We want to put one in every city in Canada and truly elevate the wellness of our country.

I'm in the best shape of my life, bills get paid, and vacations are always just around the corner. I spend my mornings drinking coffee and checking emails with my cat, going in to work when I feel ready. I live downtown and have a nice TV, but I don't really watch it. There are just too many exciting things to do.

A lot of people ask me how I have the time to do all of the things I do. I'm a meditation instructor, nutrition coach, business owner, professional fighter, Muay Thai instructor, and much more. "It's easy," I say. "I don't find time, I *make* it." I make time every day to do exciting things I love to do.

As I write this book, I find myself conflicted about the business of the book itself. How will I get it to people? Will I sell a lot of copies, or will I give them away? Will I be devaluing it by giving it away for free? These are big questions for me. So here's what I ask of you: no matter how you came across this book, let it move something within you. You don't have to believe anything I've written; in fact, I'm sure many of you won't. But at least let it stimulate you; let it shake you up a bit. Go out and work your ass off to prove me wrong. A few days of research will yield a lot of information. Maybe the answer isn't actually an answer at all, but the identification of a bigger question. Either way, you have to be willing to ask.

If you do decide to practice these concepts and see what they can offer you, make sure you see it through. Give it everything you've got—more than you've ever given. It will pay off. Mountains will move for you, but you have to be completely sure you want it. Remember the sprouting seed and leave the soil alone.

We live in the information age. I didn't write this book as the product of some wild imagination. The research is there for the taking, and everything you desire is closer to your grasp than ever in history. Everything you could ever imagine is right out there waiting for you, hidden in the cosmos. Listen to the voice inside—it is steering you exactly where you need to be.

To be as clear as I possibly can, these ideas are as real as you'll allow them to be. Please take a chance on it. Do yourself and everyone around you a favor, and just go for it, no matter what happens. I promise, if you have humility, stay humble, work hard, and follow your heart, you *cannot fail*.

I'm sending you love, gratitude, and good intentions for making the time to read my book and for taking the next step toward a rollercoaster of a life that's about to leave you breathless.

THE GREATS

I couldn't write a book without acknowledging some of the great teachers and leaders I've come across personally or through media such as books, articles, and videos. Here is a list, in no particular order, of The Greats.

- Napoleon Hill

- Bob Proctor

- Gregg Braden

- Alan Watts

- Jason Silva

- Esther and Jerry Hicks

- Rhonda Byrne

- Jack Canfield

- Elliott Hulse

- Will Smith

- Jim Carrey

- Oprah Winfrey

- Matt Mays

- Byron Katie

- Teal Swan

- Joe Rogan

- Jordan Pearce

- Lars Gustafsson

- Aubrey Marcus

- Josh Coleman

- Edgar Cayce

- Harold Sherman

- Robert Kiyosaki

- Tim Ferriss

- Cynthia Sue Larson

- Krista Raisa

REFERENCES

Faye, Jan, "Copenhagen Interpretation of Quantum Mechanics", *The Stanford Encyclopedia of Philosophy* (Fall 2014 Edition), Edward N. Zalta (ed.), forthcoming URL = <http://plato.stanford.edu/archives/fall2014/entries/qm-copenhagen/>.

Mitchell, S. D. (2004). Preface. *Philosophy Of Science, 71*(5), 669.

Complementarity principle. (2014). In *Encyclopædia Britannica.* Retrieved from http://www.britannica.com/EBchecked/topic/129874/complementarity-principle

This translation was originally published in *Proceedings of the American Philosophical Society,* 124, 323-38. [And then appeared as Section I.11 of Part I of *Quantum Theory and Measurement* (J.A. Wheeler and W.H. Zurek, eds., Princeton university Press, New Jersey 1983).]

Carpenter, R., & Anderson, A. (2006). The death of schrodinger's cat and the consciousness-based collapse of the quantum wave-function collapse. *Annales De La Fondation Louis De Broglie, 31*(1), 45.

Feynman, Richard P.; Robert B. Leighton; Matthew Sands (1965). The Feynman Lectures on Physics, Vol. 3. US: Addison-Wesley. pp. 1.1–1.8. ISBN 0201021188.

T. Inagaki, N. Matsuda, O. Tadanaga, M. Asobe, and H. Takesue, "Entanglement distribution over 300 km of fiber," Opt. Express 21, 23241-23249 (2013).

Tegmark, M. (2003), Parallel universes. Scientific American, 41.

Made in the USA
Charleston, SC
06 October 2015